7 STEPS YOU MUST KNOW TO THRIVE WHEN SH!T HAPPENS

REVISED & UPDATED

Amazon Best Selling Author
Petros 'The Human G.P.S.' Galanoulis

7 Steps You Must Know To Thrive When Sh!t Happens

By the 'Human G.P.S.' Petros Galanoulis

Third edition-Revised and updated.

First published by Createspace (Amazon) Titled: You Got This: 7 Steps To Effectively Solving Any Crisis Faster, Better.

Copyright © 2018 Petros Galanoulis Titled: You Got This: 7 Steps To Effectively Solving Any Crisis Faster, Better.

© 2022 Petros Galanoulis titled: 7 Steps You Must Know To Thrive When Sh!t Happens

ISBN-13: 978-0-6484693-6-0
ISBN-10: 0-6484693-6-0

Petros Galanoulis has asserted his right under the Copyright, Designs and Patent Act of 1988 to be identified as the author of this work. The information in this book is the authors experience and opinion, the information is intended as informative. Neither the publisher or author can be held liable for any adverse consequences resulting from the material in this book. Permission has been sought and must always be sought to use this information and any breaches must be resolved immediately.

All rights reserved. No part of this publication may be reproduced, distributed, or transmitted in any form or by any means, including photocopying, recording, or other electronic or mechanical methods, without the prior written permission of the publisher, except in the case of brief quotations embodied in critical reviews and certain other non-commercial uses permitted by copyright law. For permission requests, write to the publisher, addressed "Attention: Permissions Coordinator," at the address below.

All enquiries: gotasec@yougotthismentlhealth.com.au

Design & typesetting: Karinya Kreations Design Studio (www.kkreations.design)

Layout and Typesetting: Working type studio, Century Gothic size 12

2nd & 3rd Ed Published By:
Petros Galanoulis
Melbourne
Victoria, Australia

CONTENTS

Acknowledgments 5

Introduction 7

2 Big Things Before We Start 17

1   GATHER YOUR BEARINGS 23

    Action Items 45

2   SURVEY YOUR TERRITORY 49

    Action Items 57

3   MAP THE TERRITORY 59

    Action Items 77

4   FIND YOUR BEST PATH 83

    Action Items 89

5   CLEAR THE WAY ON THE RIGHT PATH 91

    Action Items 125

6   FORGE YOUR WAY FORWARD 139

    Action Items 145

7   ARRIVE AT YOUR DESTINATION 147

    Action Items 163

Final Thoughts 167

It Doesn't End With This Book 170

About the Author 171

Your Daily Mental Pit Stop 175

ACKNOWLEDGEMENTS

Writing a book of this nature is about sharing your life's experiences and the insights it gives you, it's also about revealing your human side to the world.

Therefore, it is right to say that the events in anyone's life have people in them that help make the experiences what they are and provide the lessons and insights in those moments.

In my life there have been numerous people that have influenced me greatly and they are:

First and foremost, my family—despite our rollercoaster relationship, I have grown so much from every dip and rise.

My friends—close, distant, current and past, you all had a part in shaping me into who I needed to be to bring this work to the world.

Past flames who helped build my heart muscle by filling it with love, breaking it, refilling it.

All the people that came into my life to annoy the crap out of me, perhaps you taught me some of the biggest lessons.

A big thank you to Karinya Sipthorp of Karinya Kreations Design Studio for the book design.

Finally, a massive thank you to Vanessa Talbot for writing my Foreword—it is indeed an honour.

A small portion of the content in this book was inspired by the work of:

- Dr Wayne Dyer,
- Anthony Robbins,
- Stephen. R. Covey, and
- Dr John Dimartini.

Although they weren't directly copied, I choose to acknowledge the influence their work had on me, my work and my book.

To all of you I give you a big and eternal...

THANK YOU

****

INTRODUCTION

Allow me to introduce myself and paint the picture of how it all came about......

I have to laugh when I think about how I got into life coaching, counselling etc and the whole personal development industry... *you might say I am the coach born from 'darkness'.*

You see, if I may get biblical for just a second, most have to walk through the fire before they find their purpose. Well, I just stumbled upon my purpose whilst I was still very much burning and in hell.

It was the 5th of July 2007, a day before my 30th birthday when I officially admitted and submitted to the fact my life was over. It was an unfixable train wreck and at this stage I hadn't even made it past the foyer of hell's castle.

I broke off the relationship I was in, a relationship that gave me my greatest gift—it turned my life upside down and finally got me to take a good look at myself.

A few years prior to that I had gone through a separation from my university sweetheart, which had meant having to get rid of the one thing that made me feel I had achieved anything... nope, not the girl—she kindly moved me on permanently—it was... my (our) house.

Five years of doing security in the worst of places, and five years more of working jobs that got me through, all hinged on this one and only symbol of all the effort I had put in.

I didn't realise how desperate and angry a human being I was and how much I was clutching at life... for life!

Yet all this happened before the real hellacious trial had even begun. You see, up to this point I hadn't even realised how mentally and emotionally messed up I was.

A little denial, a little pride and ego, a little fear perhaps made me blind to the reality. Okay—maybe a lot of denial, pride and ego, and fear, who am I kidding?

I disconnected completely from the world. At my 30th birthday what many didn't know was that they weren't looking at Petros Galanoulis, but rather a zombie version, a lifeless, hopeless, swallowed-in-darkness version of him. But the band played on, the people were merry, the well wishes flooded in and I turned 30 nonetheless. Would I see 31? Did I want to see 31?

For what seemed like forever and a day, I had only ever had a few dollars to my name, living pay cheque to pay cheque, and certainly at this time this was still true—I had quit on myself, was walking at 160kgs (I was a qualified personal trainer, which made this even worse), but nothing mattered as I walked away from that job, in fact I walked away from everything.

When I say I was disconnected, I mean in every sense: mentally, spiritually, emotionally and physically. I was literally a pathetic shell of a human being.

All this fear and anger began to affect me physically. There was your standard low energy, loss of will to live, skin irritation and weight gain but the biggest issue was a liver that wasn't quite functioning properly... it was getting fattier and fattier.

This was certainly a cold slap in the face, big enough to get me to pay some attention and try and do something about it. I began working out and eating better. I went through a series of blood tests, but the liver wasn't having a bar of it... it was hopeless.

I was fuming at this point, more than I already was if that was possible, I just couldn't see a way out, this was another slap in the face from life.

It was at this stage I discovered what *Purgatory* was like. I couldn't move forward and out of this nightmare, didn't know how, didn't have the strength; I thought about ending it all but was too much of a coward to do that, I had failed in life and now I'd failed at death, so I was left in Purgatory, neither here nor there, not anywhere.

The strangest thing was only now about to happen!

I became very private. I wasn't as social as I once was—I went into my head and that's where I sat, not wanting to come out.

I certainly exuded an energy that said stay away, I am of no use to anyone, I want to be left alone, which is why what started to happen was very bizarre, even in the midst of everything I was going through.

It started with a few friends, then some colleagues... people were coming to me for advice!!!

I even had a few people come up to me to talk about how they were depressed and anxious. In fact, one colleague came to me on a day where I had actually had an anxiety attack on the train to work.

You want to talk depression and anxiety, I could write a series of books on that one buddy... yet the truth remains, people were coming to me for advice.

Well, I was not kidding when I said I was not interested in other people, so when these misguided people came to me and asked me questions, I would tell them the very first thought and feeling that would come to me, just to get them off my back.

The sooner the conversation ended, the sooner I could go back to brooding in my head.

Well... that's not quite what happened. You see the bizarre became even more bizarre when these same people would come back to me a day or a few days or a week later to—*get this*—thank me for my advice because it helped them, it turned their situation around.

I really didn't think there was room to do my head in anymore, but I was wrong. This feedback in response to my alleged great advice was really doing a number on me; it just didn't make any sense.

One question lead to another, which lead to another...

This really got me thinking. What was it about what I had said that worked for these people? HOW HAD THIS HAPPENDED, FOR GOD'S SAKE?!!!!!

This question kept playing over and over in my head. I couldn't walk away from it. Don't get me wrong, I was still very much lost and clueless as to what to do, so I figured if I just kept helping and 'coaching' others, sooner or later I'd figure out something to do... *and so a coach was born out of the darkness... I just didn't realise it quite yet.*

By this stage I was starting to get into reading books of a spiritual and personal development nature. I was devouring five books at a time. Initially all they did was give me some comfort and solace but over time something more came from them.

I found myself getting immersed—happily—into what I was reading. I read a library of all the greats: Robbins, Dyer, Paramahansa, Buddha, Chopra, to name just a few. It wasn't just what they had written, it was the fact that so much of it resonated with me and I had an understanding, in fact a knowing, beyond anything I could explain.

For the first time in what was by this stage three years, I felt inspired and in that moment realised all I had to do was to keep asking the right questions and these *would navigate me to my desired destination*, even if at the time I wasn't sure what or where that was.

I kept devouring teachings, I kept coaching others, I just loved it, I felt alive and authentic, I felt... *meaningful and on purpose.*

Finally, someone asked me, *have you thought of becoming a life coach? A life coach?* I asked. *Yes, you are so good at it and it's clear you love it too.*

Well after my ego cooled down, I really thought about it and that week I looked up the best institution offering these types of studies and began completing my qualifications. Now I was a conscious life coach being born in the light.

At this point, I had also started my studies in Vedanta, an Indian spiritual philosophy that I hail as truly helping me awaken. I did this for two and a half years.

Don't get me wrong, I wasn't quite out of the woods as yet, but I had got into a groove. I had a system, I was coming back to life, my liver was clearing up, I had dropped 20kgs, my anxiety had disappeared, and I had found meaning and purpose... I had life, perhaps for the first time ever.

So what did I do? How did I get out of hell?

This system that I used to get out of Purgatory is the same system I predominantly use with all my clients as a personal crisis coach and myself; however, until a few years ago I never thought of it as a system. A good friend and former business partner pointed out to me that my system was so powerful and effective and asked why I wasn't promoting it better.

Well, I had never thought of it... I had never realised I had an actual, legitimate system. She eagerly described to me how she viewed my system, both as an observer and as someone who had been through it.

All that was left was to give it a name... The G.P.S system!..........Cool right?!

What exactly is it? How does it work and how did it get me and many others out of Purgatory? Well, to find the answers to these and many more questions, you will have to read on... and be prepared to get out of your head and dive headfirst into life as you have never known it before.

What is The G.P.S system?

I don't believe anyone needs to be a victim; I believe *the victim mentality* is a powerful illusion that places a veil over many people's eyes fooling them into a sense of hopelessness.

I believe we all have a navigation system within us and by unlocking it and connecting to it, we can uncover our G.P.S. – Grand Purpose of the Soul.

Not only that, I believe by connecting to our G.P.S., whether a grand purpose or simply defining an ideal outcome in a day-to-day matter, we can work our way out of any situation.

Our navigation system acts as a beacon when we are in the dark or lost or wondering what the next move is. It works by connecting us to our authenticity and truth, it helps clear the illusions imposed by or collected from society and from all the roles we play in life.

It silences all the excess noise in our head and helps us stand clearer and more focussed, and on a more stable

What is it exactly?

The G.P.S. system is about navigating your way through your mind and your obstacles and paving a path towards success in whatever you do. It's also about mastering the ability to get out of your own head and be effectively objective in any situation. There is an emphasis on asking effective and appropriate questions that lead to answers that take you to a desired destination (also known as an outcome).

Often in life there are dark spots you need to navigate through, so the G.P.S. system is like your own personal compass that helps you avoid the rocks as you sail through the ocean of life.

There is an important undertone with the G.P.S. system that says you must connect or reconnect with your authentic self because only then can you truly tap into your internal guiding system.

Once you tap into your authentic self, you can begin your journey to true fulfilment in your life, to understanding what you want from moment to moment. From the smallest moments to the largest, they all become and feel amazing and navigable.

The G.P.S. will help you to make better and more proactive decisions in your life. In this hectic world you are constantly having to make decisions, **so making the best ones for yourself is critical.**

Many things govern us in life but few as powerfully as our emotions. Our emotions can make or break us, so mastering them is a critical element of the G.P.S. system.

As you develop your sense of self and make better decisions, you are able to better define yourself. Once you can do that, you become a person of influence. The G.P.S. system helps you to become a person with influence, a true leader and a master of your emotions and your life.

With the G.P.S. system, you will find that the veil of *the victim mentality* will lift from over you, your confidence will grow and you will be able to smash through the physical and emotional barriers in your life.

The G.P.S. system is about practical and effective self-mastery and finding your **G**reatest **P**ath *to* **S**uccess in today's real world!

Whether you are an individual, a group or a business, you can apply these principles.

Whether you are resolving a minor issue at work or at home or a personal/spiritual crisis or looking to continue a streak of success, the G.P.S. system is about navigating you to a desired destination or result in 7 practical steps that can be applied to real life… to your life.

2 BIG THINGS BEFORE WE START

<u>One:</u> State of mind-your greatest ally or greatest enemy.

I'll never forget the first time I got fired……yes, there were a couple more afterwards, but they were only human and didn't know any better, I digress with my biased recollections. I was absolutely furious, my honour was besmirched, *"who the hell did my boss think he is"*?

When I got home that afternoon I could not stop pacing up and down, playing the tragedy of the day over and over again re-enacting different things I said, would've said had I thought of them at the time.

Later that evening my partner arrived home only to find me in a dishevelled state feeling sorry for myself. I explained what had happened and assured her I would look for a job right away.

She persuaded me not to do anything that night, just have dinner and relax as much as possible, she convinced me to start the job hunt the next day.

WHY WAS THAT SO IMPORTANT? Well, here is why, firstly, I was feeling anger and dissatisfaction at a boss figure, most important to me at the time was the fact that the time, blood sweat and tears I had sacrificed at that place was not appreciated.

Secondly, I was looking to unload my frustration which meant I was not thinking straight, my sense of self value was low so I wouldn't even have been able to write a decent resume.

Any attempt to find a new job would have been doomed to failure before I'd even started, which would only have enflamed my negative feelings.

What would have changed enough after a good night's sleep is my state of mind or mind set. I still would have been disappointed, but I would have had enough time to settle myself and start thinking a little clearer.

Our mind set or state of mind acts like a kind of filter, a filter on how we see things, think of it as a clip-on camera lens, if it's the wrong lens we don't see things clearly and therefore make mistakes and vice versa.

I was once told quite wisely never make any major decisions when you are highly excited and elated or depressed, I quickly realised that in both those states we aren't at our clearest, we are drunk or blinded by our emotions which have us in an extreme state.

Being in such an extreme state is like having an overly powerful lens on your camera, you don't see things with proper clarity and balance.

Can you think of a time where you were feeling down, defeated and tried to make an important decision and decided far less effectively than what you would have had you waited a day or two?

It's important therefore that we maintain awareness of our mood or state of mind and understand what is the cause behind it? The reason for this is it's important to deal with and bring some clarity about your state of mind so as to centre you somewhat and to bring your awareness that there is something that may prevent you from seeing clearly and balanced therefore detrimentally affecting your ability to make appropriate and positively effective decisions.

So how do we manage our state of mind and prevent it from intoxicating the decisions we make? Let's start exploring that now.

Two: **When things just don't go your way....** **And sometimes they won't!**

Sometimes the universal joo joo doesn't flow your way, the eternal current blows it the other way and no matter what you do you just can't catch a break, such is the reality of life for all.

Can you recall a time where things just weren't going your way and somehow no matter what you did it just made things worse?

Well, this is because everything you did was from the position of trying to take back control and force change. This is natural, you are a responsible human being, you take charge and responsibility of your life.

Here is the kicker, sometimes the most responsible and adult thing to do is nothing, simply recognize that things aren't going your way and let the wind of change ride itself out.

As humans we instinctively act to gain control and put ourselves above a situation, it's part of our need for certainty and survival and to move from pain to pleasure, however in doing so we make things worse.

I remember when I ran an online cigar store it was 2009 it was coming up to elections in Australia and the government at the time decided that the way it was going to try and win extra votes was to start a crusade on tobacco products.

Ridiculous new laws were introduced and measures that made no sense other than revenue raising were rolled out which made many organisations such as Pay Pal put a ban, without warning, on all tobacco products which one Wednesday morning left me without a merchant service.

Well, you can imagine my mood at the time, I started with calling PayPal and screaming the life out of them, all that did was attract multiple hang ups, I began ringing other third-party merchant services who also rejected me.

I had to do something, so I switched the pay options on my site to bank transfer and put up my bank details but in doing so I somehow crashed my site which meant a few hours on the phone to tech support who felt more like a hindrance than support.

This day just kept going from bad to worse and no matter what I just couldn't do anything right.

Eventually the next day I set up a portable card reader with one of our major banks, I could take credit card details safely as normal but would have to manually input every order from then on. Not ideal but better than nothing.

Compare that to the last 6 months of 2015, they turned a year that started one way into the complete opposite. There was a long-term project that I had to let go because after 3 years it just wasn't getting to where I'd hoped it would, I'd lost a little bit of direction with where I wanted to go business wise and with my coaching service which meant I wasn't attracting enough of the clients I wanted or the right ones. I truly felt I had hit a brick wall mentally, physically and most importantly spiritually.

But I knew better this time, I knew that when things aren't going your way it's because:

    a) The universe is making preparations for your next stage and progression and

    b) Because it's a good time to reflect, assess and determine what needs replacing, changing, re-visioning and finally

    c) Because you are just meant to sit with things and do nothing in particular for a while.

Knowing this I didn't fight or resist in this case I let things be and 2 things happened, I got the clarity and true direction for where to take my business to and with that I created two new workshop seminars which I am so excited about and gained better clientele.

Both scenarios were difficult and a case of nothing good coming my way, in fact the second incident lasted months not a day yet two totally different outcomes.

Why? Awareness, when things aren't going your way that's ok, just remember you just need to be aware and let things be, go about the best you can as oppose to trying to force the change, I promise you things do get better.

Utilise this time to review things and seek better ways if possible or at least understand it's not necessarily about you and it's all part of the unfolding of life.

It's a great time to be mindful and objective till the wave runs out, and when it does, and you have allowed things to be and reviewed, reflected, been mindful and objective, you will find yourself at the end further ahead than you could have imagined, even if just emotionally and mentally.

1

GATHER YOUR BEARINGS – WHERE ARE YOU PRECISELY?

Seeing it from inside your head, what exactly and specifically is the crisis as you see it right now?

"Oooh I am so mad! He absolutely stabbed me in the back, now my world is falling apart at the seams."

"I want to get that position, but I am probably not quite qualified enough to get it!"

Ever made a dramatic statement such as that? Did your world fall apart at the seams? What do seams on a world look like? Or maybe you went for that job anyway and found out it wasn't so out of your reach.

So often you become so dramatic and emotional in situations that you end up making grand and broad comments, which can often dictate your situation.

You can also get lost in the emotions and reactions because they are too much to reconcile. This confusion may hide the fact that you might not be very clear on what exactly the problem is and you may also feel helpless or settle for less, unnecessarily.

However, is there some sense in making these grand, emotional and dramatic statements?

Yes! There is definitely more than meets the eye to these outbursts. They are your view of whatever has happened or is occurring in its rawest form.

These comments are reflective of your most primal level feelings and emotions and, as we will explore later in this book, they give you clues on how to act based on whatever is happening in that moment.

Venting does have some purpose and it's good to get things out of your system the right way in order to move forward.

The effects of venting are more than just letting off some steam, there are also physical effects that venting can help us with leading us to healing.

The Power Of A Good Vent

One of the Top 3 causes of disease is a *destructive mindset and negativity*.

Why are our thoughts, our state of mind so important to our health and wellbeing? Why is it that the most devastating causes of disease are our thoughts and mindsets and yet they can also heal even cancer?

Amazing things happen in our bodies when we think. Firstly, thoughts are conscious energy (I will cover conscious energy in more detail further on), and thoughts are measurable. They are measured by a process called Positron Emission Tomography (P.E.T.), which monitors the effects of the thought energy and the biochemical reactions in our central nervous system generated by our thoughts.

We now know for a fact what the ancients knew over 5000 years ago—how and what we think generates our reality and releases different types of chemicals in our body creating varying states of **well-being** and or **disease**.

When you are having positive-oriented and hopeful thoughts and are maintaining a balanced and happy outlook, you have a high production of:

- Endorphin – the body's natural painkiller and healer, 30 times more powerful than morphine.

- Serotonin – a chemical that helps maintain a 'happy feeling' and helps keep our moods under control by helping with sleep, calming anxiety and relieving depression.

- Dopamine – which makes people more talkative and excitable, it affects brain processes that control movement, emotional response and ability to experience pleasure and pain.

These three hormones amongst many help regulate your body and your sense of feeling and wellbeing.

Therefore, keeping your frustrations or ill feelings bottled up is poisonous because it creates a state of anxiety, panic and more negative thinking, etc., which leads to the reduction of your happy hormones.

Reduced serotonin and endorphin leads to an increase in depression and anxiety, and reduced resistance of the body towards pain and illness.

Reduced serotonin also increases addictive behaviour and increases risk of heart disease and diabetes. When you are low on the good hormones, your body, including your heart, functions irregularly.

When your body functions irregularly, you see an increase in cortisol—a catabolic (stress) hormone, your internal environment becomes a breeding ground for illnesses such as cancer, which requires an environment in dis-ease to manifest and grow.

So, when you vent, you are releasing pressure, pressure that can have harmful effects on your body if kept in.

Another effect of venting is that it can clear your mind and help you to think more proactively when engaged in a situation, regardless of whether it is a positive or a negative scenario. This occurs because we switch from the amygdala in the lower lateral part of the brain where our fight or flight system resides, to the prefrontal cortex which is roughly our forehead, where our executive functions reside.

Now venting has its do's and don'ts and many vent negatively, in fact destructively I would say.

When you are venting and expressing what has happened and you are stating it with all your emotions, judgments, and prejudices, you are taking the **'subjective'** view.

The subjective view is a view purely based on yourself, what you think should have been and what you want and what happened.

There is nothing wrong with that until you have expectations that everything should be as you want it and should revolve around you.

This is limiting and delusional and can be a little obnoxious; however even worse than that, it can be restrictive and outright debilitating.

The reason for this is it blinds you to the potential possibilities and realities of a situation, which means you don't see potential solutions and benefits in your day-to-day life or in any situation. This happens because subconsciously you set out to prove yourself right.

So here is what to do…

I encourage you here to *just let it out, no matter how profane or dramatic it may be*, just get it off your chest privately and with no chance of harm to anyone or negative outcome, do it with an open mind and even with a venting buddy, *then journal it.*

WHAT! Journaling?

In a space of three years, between 2007 and 2010, I filled up eight journals. It was a time where I had a lot of soul searching to do and things to figure out.

As a thinker, it was great to write things down—it cleared my head and allowed insight and guidance to come through. It meant I could also focus on something else rather than being consumed by my thoughts.

Journaling allows you to view your thoughts better, and with more clarity, and you don't have to remember them as you can come back to them in the journal.
This also allows you to step back and look at the situation with more perspective.

The act of writing out your thoughts also inspires creativity and the flow of thoughts and ideas, which is critical to progress and healing. Journaling is great for uncovering your best next move; these are actions that when delivered to you, must be taken, as they are essential to your overall journey to success in life.

Journalling is also a great way of calming our Vagal nerve, which is a network of nerves that fire up when we are feeling stressed.

For this to work, you must dedicate a few minutes either each day or every second or third day (whatever you can manage) where you find a quiet and comfortable place to write down your thoughts.

When you have let it all out, the first thing you must do in finding your way in a situation is to gather your bearings, get clear on what exactly and specifically is the challenge/situation as you see it now.

The First Step To Becoming Clear Is:

Checking Your Beliefs

You must come to understand what your beliefs are about the situation.

Get precise, right down to everything you believe about the situation—what it is, what the cause is and what the effect is, as well as potential outcomes.

Be clear about where you feel you are at right now.

The Truth About Beliefs

Defining what a belief is: A belief is a feeling of *certainty* about something.

How a belief is formed
The five characteristics of a belief:

1) *There was an event/trigger:* You heard, experienced or saw something that triggered a sensation and/or reaction of some sort.

2) *Your level of knowledge, experience, awareness at the time begins to form your opinion:* You resolve that moment, event, experience, etc., based on what you know, your level of intelligence at that point in time.

3) *You make a determination (opinion):* Based on the above two points, you draw your conclusions and sort through them till you find the one that you feel makes most sense to you.

4) *You then decide that this determination is fact:* When you find the conclusion that feels most right, you cross reference it in your mind's filing system, and when you can't find an alternative explanation, you determine that this conclusion is fact.

5) *You feel certain:* Once you have labelled your determination as fact, you become certain, and so a belief is born. You start to live and defend it.

Beliefs are very powerful, for they can determine how you *live* and how you *behave* towards yourself and others.

They can lift you up or blind you to your own detriment, therefore it is important that you keep an open mind and review your beliefs often.

Three reasons why beliefs are so powerful:

1) They can have both physiological and psychological effects on you.

2) They can move you forward or hold you back and outright destroy you – e.g. the champion vs. the suicide victim, both are mentalities based on beliefs.

3) They can activate the RAS in your brain, which is the part of your brain where subconscious thought is stored and created and where all the information you

receive consciously and otherwise is processed. Activating the RAS is also how your brain subconsciously seeks proof of your belief, despite there being plenty of evidence to the contrary.

Um... The... RAS?!!

The R.A.S. – Reticular Activation System

When you see, you see with your brain and not with your eyes; through the sense organs and the nerves in your brain, the data you receive is then converted into images which you perceive and experience.

That perception also varies between your conscious brain and unconscious brain or your conscious mind and subconscious mind.

You process over 300 billion bits of information daily but you are not aware of all of that information. In fact, you are conscious of maybe 1,000,000 bits of information and use an even smaller portion of that as it suits you.

Your decisions are made in micro-seconds every moment of your life, awake or asleep, and what you focus on is determined or controlled by the RAS.

The RAS is a bunch of nerve pathways that sit at the base of your brain linking to your spinal cord and cerebrum. It basically acts as a filter for all external input that is picked up from your everyday external life.

The RAS is like a net that catches everything, in fact *reticular* is Latin for 'little net'. It collects everything that comes at you and allocates it to the appropriate part of your brain, creating your various sensations, etc.

Think of it as the bouncer at the front door of a club and your brain is the night club. The guard chooses who comes in and who stays out, who is a V.I.P.

Consider a time when you were in a crowd. There would have been thousands of sounds, but none were of any real significance. Suddenly you hear the call of your mother or your significant other in the crowd and can home in on that above all other noise and distractions.

That sound resonated with information you had stored in your mind that was a representation of something you want or hold as significant and therefore it was able to get your attention.

To relate it to your beliefs, what you believe is equivalent to what you want, so you create a sequence of information in your brain that says to your RAS: seek this where possible.

If you truly believe something, you will attract it just by way of your RAS filtering everything else out and bringing to your attention that which aligns with the sequence of information in your head.

Let's use the example of a crowded, noisy place: you hear your significant other's voice and everything else is blocked out but then a voice yells 'FIRE'!!

Do you hear it or not?

Think of it like this, the voice of your significant other is your current belief about something, and the voice yelling 'FIRE' is another possibility, one that could be very important and very beneficial to you.

Being stuck in your beliefs could mean missing out on better options and this can hold you back or even harm you. Be flexible and open with your beliefs, for they are transient. It might not necessarily mean they are not true; they might just no longer be *relevant, empowering* or indeed *valid or the best option anymore*.

Many of your beliefs were learned as a child and were mimicked from those that were most influential to you during those years when you were forming your young ego.

They become so embedded in you by adulthood that you continue to carry them even if they are no longer relevant and even if deep inside you don't really believe them.

Three Reasons Why A Belief Is Transient:

1) *Your knowledge grows and changes,* you become wiser and smarter through experience. As you evolve, so does your knowledge and your insight. Clinging onto old information will stunt your growth and your chances of attracting what you want to achieve.

2) *The event/trigger can be multi-dimensional* it can have multiple perspectives and meanings. Quite often you are blinded to the many possible meanings of a situation by your feelings, expectations and so forth. This creates a sense of tunnel vision, which may prevent you from considering the bigger view of things. When

you understand this, you open yourself up to a whole lot more possibility and potential.

3) *You always have a choice* when making decisions and decisions can be changed over time as you learn more and see more. The act of changing your beliefs or becoming more *objective* is a decision, one you can make at any time.

In all areas of your life take time to ask yourself the following questions on a regular basis:

"What are my beliefs?"

"Whose are they really?"

"What do I really believe?"

"Are they serving me?"

A major part of getting clear and evolving is the ability to step out of your head and look at your beliefs from a bigger picture point of view. You need to be able to start connecting with that internal G.P.S and asking yourself what is the truth in a given situation and could what you have believed actually not be the best fit. Could there even be other possibilities?

It's learning to make positive decisions based on more than just what you think, rather based on what is the reality and the possibilities. It's being flexible in the face of infinite potentiality and under the pressure of an event or situation.

The Second Step To Being Clear Is:

Handling Your Emotions/Feelings:

"I feel flat!"

"I am so pumped up!"

Have you ever actually seen a flat person or one with a pump... um... you know, being pumped up?

You often look at your feelings and emotions from a very metaphoric point of view. They can lift you up or knock you down, so it's important to know if your emotions and feelings are serving you well or not.

In extreme moments of intense feeling, whether good or bad, we often exaggerate our emotions and feelings by the addition of drama and grandeur searing through our descriptions.

It's important to understand that your feelings/emotions are not the descriptions you give them, but instead they are messages.

Your emotions and feelings are messages that your subconscious or higher self is transmitting to you about what has really happened and what action you need to take to get to where you want and/or what you want.

Let's take a closer look at emotions...

Problems always arise, and, in the end, you don't always have to see eye to eye or agree with everyone, but nothing can be gained by holding it in and carrying it throughout your life. It's always about how you *deal with* and *handle* your emotions relating to an issue and how *responsibly* you stand.

Are you about being right or doing right? As Stephen R Covey, author of 'The 7 Habits of Highly Effective people', says: *"Seek to understand then be understood, begin with the end in mind"* and I will add:

"Always remember the greater good that truly counts in the end."

Your *emotions* determine your success in virtually everything and learning to master them is an art form that can mean the difference between *losing* your home or *making* it to the top of your field of expertise.

"I'm an emotional person, how can I control what I feel when I am feeling it"?

When we react under extreme emotion what we say, do or believe can embed itself deep into our mind, forming new neurological paths. This is how we create habits, deep beliefs which can work for us or against us, so how do we manage this?

Seven Steps To Being The Boss Of Your Emotions

1) *Identify* what you are feeling
   e.g. rejected or disappointed.

2) *Acknowledge and appreciate* your emotions knowing they support you. As you appreciate them and notice them, they will calm down.

3) *Get curious* about the true message this emotion is offering you. This is an immediate pattern interrupt that allows you to master problem solving and prevention.

4) *Get confident* – reflect to a previous time where you felt like this and got through it.

5) *Get certain* you can handle this, not only today but tomorrow as well, and have a plan, rehearse and then apply.

6) *Get excited.*

7) *Take action.*

Understanding the deeper meaning of your emotions and how you deal with them will enable you to better handle them and understand them rather than running from them or denying them; *you need to* **get real.**

Here are some basic examples of what we are really saying in some of our more primal reactions:

> 'There are four basic ways in which people deal with emotions':

1) *Avoiding the emotion:* people try to avoid situations that may lead to emotions they fear or situations where they don't feel confident and comfortable.

    Another option: learn the hidden meaning in those things you once thought were negative and see the positive in confronting what you are afraid of or uncomfortable with. Tell someone—it's the key to freedom.

2) *Denying the feelings or situation exist*: people try to disassociate from their feelings, e.g., "It's not that bad." They figure maybe it will just fix itself and go away. In other cases, people just prefer to kid themselves that anything is going on full stop

    Option: understand and use the emotions to admit and accept what you are really feeling, as that's the only thing that can be dealt with and converted to your favour.

3) *Competition – when your emotions become a point of merit:* many stop fighting their emotions and instead indulge in them, e.g., "You think you have problems, well I..." It's like a trophy, something they place on a pedestal.

Option: understand that these emotions serve a positive purpose, that there is something that needs changing or a shift of perception. All of which leads to...

4) *Taking the feedback and using it proactively:* your emotions, good or bad, are a compass that points you towards the actions you must take.

Your emotions can be your lighthouse in smooth and rough times, they can serve you as guidance from your higher self and nudge you towards what you need to be doing.

However, misunderstood or poorly framed, the light will shine dim and you may hit rocks along the way.

Embrace your emotions and feelings, observe them and enquire into them, address them appropriately and they will shine light on the best way for you to go to avoid the rocks.

"Okay, so how about if I am having a 'spirited debate' with someone or I am in a negotiation, these events can get pretty emotional and heated?"

The art of win/win is the skill of *diffusing* conflict, active or potential, and opting instead to *work together* till you find an *agreed* common ground where all sides *benefit*.

Regardless of whether it's a debate or an argument, a negotiation or just simple communication between two people, here are some tips:...

Quick and effective tips to overcoming resistance and creating solutions.

- *There's no such thing as resistance*, just inflexible communicators. Just like when you cling onto one belief, you miss out on other possibilities, the same happens when you dig in your heels and are not open to terms that benefit all parties.

- *Instead of opposing another's view, be flexible and resourceful* enough to sense the creation of resistance. You know what sets you off on a basic primal level, chances are the person opposite you is set off by the same thing. Effective communication is being able to foresee potential causes of resistance and attend to them to diffuse them, sooner rather than later.

- *Find points of agreement* with the other person; align yourself with these and redirect communications towards a win/win outcome. Following on from the above points, the goal should always be finding a point of agreement where both parties are happy and can move forward.

- *Understand certain words and phrases create resistance* and problems, hence pay attention to the words you use and the effects they have. For example, 'But' negates everything said before it, substitute the word but with 'and' and see the difference. "That's an interesting idea and here is another interesting way to think about it."
The word **'also'** is a word that encourages synergy as opposed to separation.

- *Build rapport* and keep the person open by creating a frame of agreement. This is an extension of using language that inspires progress and not resistance. For example,

    - I appreciate and…
    - I respect and…
    - I agree and…

    This acknowledges the other person's communication and respects it rather than denigrating it with **'no'**, **'but'** or **'however'**. You're building a bond and rapport and opening the door to redirecting something without resistance.

- *Redefine problems* in such a way so as both agree rather than disagree. If a conversation is becoming stagnant or repetitive or heading down an unproductive path, etc., interrupt the pattern, pick the record needle up and put it elsewhere and start afresh.

- *Pre-interrupts:* Extending on from the above point, when you think a conversation is unproductive or heated, interrupt by using humour or immediate understanding, etc. Show you are paying attention and understand the situation and the other person's position.

- *Be proactive* and *always keep your word*. Trust is the ultimate element in any relationship. If you promise something, make sure it's beneficial to all parties and make sure you deliver what you say you will.

- *Do not look at the other person as competition* or someone to conquer, instead build through agreement. Our ego has a tendency to pop up in circumstances of debate or negotiation, which makes us see the other as someone to beat as opposed to someone to work with for a greater goal. It's a selfish and, in some cases, insecure position to hold.

- *Resistance* is caused by not wanting to change and defend that which you won't change. Success is instant but whether it is or is not for you, is dependent on you.

When you are properly tuned in to your emotions and feelings, you come to quickly discover that your deepest truest feelings are your ultimate G.P.S.

Building your awareness and deciding on achieving a greater more positive outcome, beliefs + emotional mastery positively enhances the results you get in your life.

Enough talk, time for action

Action Item 1:

Check your beliefs, set a solid foundation.

Consider some of the beliefs you have in general about life or in regard to a specific situation or topic. You can come back to this task for different beliefs you want to qualify.

1. When did you first begin to have this belief, approximately?

2. What happened around that time that created this belief in you?

3. Is this belief still relevant and applicable to your life today?

4. Looking at the situation that triggered this belief through your current eyes, how could you reframe the event better, knowing what you know now?

5. If the trigger event is a current situation, what else could be plausibly true about that event?

6. With this new perspective, would you say that your belief in its current state is a positive or a negative for your success?

7. If it's a negative, and even if it's not, with your new perspective how can you improve or update your belief, so it serves you better?

Action Item 2

Start being the master of your emotions and get ahead.

Your emotions can blind you and hold you back, making you their victim. Consider an emotion you are currently battling with that is overwhelming you. Follow these six steps now and become the master of your emotions.

1. Identify what it is you are feeling exactly.

2. Looking past the initial emotion, what is the message being delivered. It's important you look at it without the emotions or judgment, like a third party observer.

3. Think of a previous time you had a similar situation, what were the negative patterns, and what did you do to interrupt them and get you back onto a positive path?

4. Knowing you can handle this, make a plan for getting through the particular situation. Give some thought to what matters and what you need in this case.

5. Take action-What's your first move, when will you do it?

Once you are able to properly communicate the challenge you are facing, and manage the beliefs and feelings, you can then begin to...

2

SURVEY YOUR TERRITORY

Getting out of your head, now you can start being more objective and practical about the challenge/situation, so as to find the messages and truth behind it.

> "Oh, that wasn't quite as bad as I thought."

Ever said that before?

Once you can become clear on the situation/challenge and what you feel and believe, you can then begin to truly see the situation as it really is, not better or worse.

We have a tendency to make things personal when something happens to us and this can happen both when good and bad things happen.

Consider these examples:

> A bad situation may be when you are at the supermarket and you head over to the bakery to buy some bread rolls and, as you approach the bread roll shelf, another person strolls by and grabs the last pack of bread rolls. Now, you would likely swear that person saw you going for the bread rolls and took them from you!
>
> How dare they take your bread rolls? You need them to make hot dogs tonight. Have they no decency? How dare they take your bread rolls and deny you your hot dogs?

Does that sound familiar? More importantly, does it sound a little unrealistic and melodramatic? Could there be another explanation, a truer reality?

> A good situation may be a time when you have been working hard on a project that resulted in helping your team achieve certain targets more easily and

efficiently. In your mind you were hoping for a full ceremony for your efforts, instead you got a pat on the back and everyone went about their work.

"How can they ignore me and my efforts like that?" you think to yourself. After all you put so much time and energy, so much passion into it. Don't they care?

Is this a familiar situation? Again, is there a more realistic or more practical explanation?

Don't get me wrong, some situations can be personal but even in those moments you have a choice as to whether you do or don't take them personally.

When you clear away the fog and become more certain, more confident, you can then properly face and understand your situation/challenge and *take ownership* of it.

The critical step to being more accurate is to:

Sift The Facts From The Drama:

Make your proclamation

A proclamation is an official announcement, often these are made publicly but in the context of this book we shall say it's the official acceptance of your situation, by way of stating the reality, you are making a statement of truth.

You can't start to deal with any challenge or situation until you admit it exists.

However, just admitting it exists is not, on its own, enough. You need to admit the *reality and/or truth of your situation as it stands right now*.

This means you need to understand what you need to accept about this situation, whether you like it or not. The difference between this and just getting it off your chest is that now you are removing your own judgement and prejudice from the situation.

This means reviewing the situation as a neutral observer and stating the same situation honestly and objectively minus your attachment to the situation and switching to a proactive mindset.

This primes you for solution and success rather than perpetuating the problem and the behaviour that lead to it. What has happened has happened and it cannot be rewritten. No amount of wishing or pissing and moaning will make it… undone. **I've tried that!**

Get a load off your back

Now that you have decided not to struggle with the reality of your situation, you are ready to frame your acceptance and realisation in the form of a factual statement.

For example: "John completely screwed me over when he lost my paperwork!" *becomes:* The paperwork was lost by John and I need to get fresh copies.

Which one is easier to step up to and deal with?

The idea here is rather than getting caught up in your situation, you allow yourself to step out of it for a moment and become the *'observer'*. This will give you a bigger and better perspective on the whole picture and it's easier not to get personal and blur your judgement.

When you finally speak out and release the truth, it's like letting the steam out from a pressure cooker, it's a massive relief.

It is important when you state your challenge that you:

1) Embrace it; it's a part of your journey, moulding you into becoming a greater and stronger person.

2) Speak factually and neutrally, free from emotions, assumptions and accusations.

3) Be realistic and proactive in your proclamation.

As you develop a more proactive view of your situation, you can begin to put it into one of three categories of classification.

I define situations as one of three types:

1) Communication/Relationship-based

2) Decision-based

3) Personal Internal-based.

Now some situations may overlap, in which case you can either determine whether your situation falls predominantly into one classification over the other, or it may simply be the case that your situation is an equal combination of all three classifications.

It really doesn't matter, as these classifications are more of a guide towards discovering what type of challenge your current situation is.

Let's take a closer look at these classifications...

The 3 Types Of Situations We Are Faced With Daily

1) Communication/Relationship-based matters

These are situations that involve another person, whether it's someone close to you, such as a friend, intimate partner or family member, or a colleague, stranger, business associate, etc.

In these matters there is either an action that has been taken or an action that is wanted or needed to be taken that involves you and another.
In all cases the lowest common denominator is communication; how you do it both in your own head and with the other person (or persons) will determine the direction, meaning and outcome of

Tips: *Allow for emotions to settle and get clear on what you want and what you are willing to do to help achieve the outcome you want,*

2) Decision-based matters

Situations of decision are situations where you aren't sure which way you want to go.

This is often described as procrastination. Think of a time when you had a choice to make and just weren't sure which choice to go with.

Often you may find yourself at a crossroads in a given situation and your decision indicates which path to take.

Tips: *Here is where you need to work with logic and facts, if you are unsure then consider what information you need, list where you can obtain it with quickest/ easiest route first then take action, work to a plan.*

3) Personal Internal-based matters

   A personal internal matter is when you find yourself at a deeper crossroads. An internal matter could be something such as understanding who you are, what direction you want in your life or resolving your position and what to do about a matter of deep moral or character defining or life affecting.

   Tip: *Time is important here to give to yourself as is permission to feel, connect with and be positively selfish. It's important to give yourself permission to attend to you. Arrive to your outcome naturally and authentically.*

   Placing your situation under one or more of these categories helps to further clarify your situation. The more this is done, the better you can begin to deal with it.

Enough talk, time for action

Action Item 1:

An exercise in getting out of your head and onto higher ground to achieve the best outcomes.

Take any situation that may be a challenge and may be pushing you and follow these steps:

1. Make your proclamation, have a good vent and state out loud what the situation is and how you feel about it with all your emotions and judgments. Let it all out.

2. Reframe the same situation again, this time factually and truthfully minus the emotions, judgments and personal positions, like an observer.

3. Is the situation:
   a) decision,
   b) communication/relationship or
   c) personal internal as per the descriptions on previous page?

4. With this fresh view of your situation, what are three better more proactive ways you can approach your situation?

Once you have made your proclamation and surveyed your territory you can then proceed to...

3

MAP THE TERRITORY

Beginning to understand the elements and possibilities of your situation/challenge fully.

Once you have realised and accepted your situation/challenge and proclaimed it, you must now start to turn it around.

Ever tried eating a burger in one bite? Does that work? Safe to say, no it does not. You would do yourself some serious discomfort if you tried...

Please do not try that.

It's the same with any situation you face, especially the challenging ones. You look at problems as one singular thing and try to 'devour' that one whole thing and you're overwhelmed as soon as you try that.

Like your burger, it just can't be done. Certain elements came together to create your situation, which means that, like a burger, your situation has more than one part to it.

To resolve something, you must break it down and truly understand that a situation is rarely made up of one element.

There are a series of events, factors that lead to a situation being what and how it is and its critical we acknowledge that fact and the elements themselves.

This serves a number of purposes including the most important one, positively solving the challenge.

The First Step To Understanding The Elements:

Break The Situation Down In To Its Parts:

Take your situation and look at it carefully. Identify the elements that make up the whole situation. For example:

The situation: *"John completely screwed me over when he lost my paperwork!"*

First element: *John had the paperwork*
Second element: *The paperwork was lost by John.*
Third element: *He screwed me over.*
Fourth element: *(Insinuated) I am in a position of disadvantage.*

A great way to find the elements of a situation is to simply picture yourself describing that situation as a *play by play* to another person. This will help you break down the situation. Remember you are doing it as an impartial observer.

Once you have the elements, determine what classification of situation it is: *Communication/ Relationship, Decision or Personal Internal.*

In this situation, as you see it initially, there are four elements to the situation/challenge and, in this example, it's a communication/relationship issue.

The Second Step To Understanding The Elements:

Break Down Your Feelings:

I have found when working with clients that many understand the concept of breaking down the situation but very few break down their feelings to understand the real message behind them, or to truly understand their representation.

Your feelings and thoughts are linked; how you react, receive and perceive your situation will determine if you understand it and how you act.

So, it is critical to apply this breakdown process to your feelings/emotions.

This can be easily achieved with one simple question:

What are all the sensations and images going through my head, through my heart and my gut?

Now in positive situations, you can follow this process as well, to understand the elements that lead to your moments of success and happiness and how it was achieved, how you led yourself to that moment of bliss.

You can then document and apply these elements consistently in your life and perpetuate positivity and success in your life daily.

Then there maybe situations surrounding just a feeling you may have, or you may have made some decisions that are causing some discomfort or a sense of uncertainty.

The Power of Images and Symbols

I remember a time when I was having problems at work. I felt that I was being overlooked by management, which frustrated me a lot.

I started having images of my managers in a room with me, while I tore them apart and brought out what I felt were their weaknesses.

Now at face value, you might think I wanted to put my managers down and cause them harm but the reality is slightly different... thankfully.

The reality is that my physical actions in my thoughts represented the values in me I felt had been violated. In this case, I felt trust had been broken, I felt unacknowledged for the time and effort I had put in, I felt a lack of appreciation.

The verbal aspect represented frustration and my own inability to figure out what I needed to do. The words or, more to the point, the criticisms of them I was highlighting in my thoughts were really the subconscious realisation of my own insecurities and weaknesses, which were irritated by my situation.

By studying these images and symbols and delving deeper into what they could mean, I was able to review my situation and take a newer, more proactive and effective approach.

Now it doesn't stop there. You have been blessed with many tools and abilities to help you navigate through life.

This next factor is a powerful one as it helps you really pinpoint where your concerns lie, what *position they are in*.

To better understand these feelings, we must look at what I have coined:
Proximity of Feelings

Proximity of feelings is a concept I came up with after working with numerous clients, where I realised that feelings can be placed in a position within a certain proximity from you, along an event continuum which can better shed some light on where your actual concerns are.

> 'Our feelings can be physical markers indicating where our problem actually lies'.

For example, the feeling may be, I have decided to quit my job to start my own business, and now I feel doubtful about whether I did the right thing.

Question: Does the doubt feel like it's behind you? Is it way In front of you? Or close in front of you? You may also have visions of looking over your shoulder, way ahead of you or beside you.

Interpretations: *If you find the feelings feel like they are behind you,* it means that you are unsure if you decided correctly or went the right way about starting your new venture.

If you find that the feelings are ahead of you, it may reflect your own doubt and lack of confidence to survive without a job and build a business. You are unsure how to finish and launch.

If you find that the feelings are in front but close or beside you, it may mean that, although it's the right decision, you are unsure of where to start and move forward and so you're feeling a little low on confidence or momentarily lost.

Now these are very general explanations, but this task is about understanding where the problem lies, owning your situation and tackling it from a position of centeredness, and in the best possible mindset for the best possible outcome.

The Two Most Common Emotional Blockages and What They Really Mean

Fear and Limitation

1-Fear is a powerful phenomenon that can hold people back and downright cripple them in their life and perhaps it's the true ultimate killer of dreams. But what is fear really?

False-**E**vents-**A**ppearing-**R**eal - Fear is the art of creating a story in your mind, or a version of events in which:

    a) That's how it will be
    b) That's the only way it can be
    c) You are hopeless in this situation.

Essentially fear is just a story, a false sense of certainty that rarely, if ever, is as you imagine it. *It is only because that's how we decided it will be, not because that's how it definitely is.*

The fear you feel can be an indication of what you focus on the most and/or a reflection of your insecurities. This fear can be blinding and not only limit you, but also make you feel you are completely limited without possibility or options.

Your sense of limitation is what fear uses to paralyse you and keep you in hopelessness and inaction, but what really are limitations and what can we do about them?

2-A Sense of Limitation – quite often one of the biggest creators of fear is limitation, perceived or actual.

Limitations are where your *knowingness* and your *unknowingness meet*. This boundary is transient, non-permanent, you have pushed it, expanded on it all your life and this never changes. Both of these blockers are illusions that cause you to procrastinate.

Procrastination is when you either can't or won't decide or keep putting a decision off. The ultimate weapon against fear and limitations is the consistent development of knowledge and the relentless taking of action on that knowledge until you are comfortable and no longer fearful of that situation or event.

Fear and limitations get in your face, blocking your view of the truth of your situation – you are not victims or helpless, nor is this the only possibility or definition of an event, no matter what.

They fool you into accepting and settling on the fact that the way things are is it, when all you need to do is acknowledge that the fear is there and move on to beating it. Fear can prevent you from doing the things you need to do to overcome it and achieve your goals.
Fear says you need security not freedom. Fear says go with what you know; it is safe even if you are miserable. We create a dependence on security and live in fear of losing it.

Can Fear Have A Positive Effect?

Yes, it can have two positive effects if you <u>do not let it take over</u>:

1) It serves to keep your head out of the clouds and stops you taking unnecessary and/or stupid risks.

2) It can be the fuel, the push you need to take action. In the face of defeat, it can be the elastic that catapults you forward when there is nothing left to lose and everything to gain.

We are creatures with an ego. It varies from person to person and one of the ego's greatest needs is the need to be right, even in the face of evidence suggesting otherwise. So fear and limitations will use this to fool you and make you focus on the wrong things.

Consider for a moment that everything is energy; your thoughts are energy, you are energy, in fact the only thing that separates you from a tree is the vibrational frequency of your energies. You vibrate differently to a tree, which vibrates differently to a rock, and this is why there are many infinite forms and creations in the world.

The thing about energy is it's a magnet to <u>like</u> energies. This means if you are thinking and acting one way, you vibrate a certain way and so attract more of that into your life, into your consciousness.

It's important to check in with your thoughts and feelings, stories and excuses to make sure you're not developing an inner and outer world contrary to your goals and who you want to be.

The great news is you control what you think about and what you decide; no other thing or person can do this for you, *at least not without your permission!!*

The Power of Words

They say the pen is mightier than the sword, truth be told a greater truth cannot be spoken.

The sword is clear and swift, it hurts whilst the wound is upon you agape, as it heals so does the pain go away but words, they can be unforgivingly harsh, swift or slow and calculated and the pain can linger a lifetime.

Words have the power to create law, to bring down empires to empower and free a person or imprison them and render them incapable.

No greater adversary as they who use words as their weapon, exist than our self which makes what we say, how we say it and to whom a matter of life or potential death.

Our words can and often if not always are a reflection of our inner environment, our relationship with ourselves and inevitably the world around us, words can also create truths, truths that can either empower us or sabotage us. We have the choice if aware of it but even then there are no guarantees.
The words we use and attitudes we have on a consistent basis can and do bring our focus upon the strongest theme in those words. Now consider for a moment that 90% of our thinking is done in our subconscious as a result of what we focus on the most, then the words we use consistently become critical to our quality of life and our chances of success and happiness.

The mechanics of this I explain in detail in the section about the RAS-Reticular Activation System. It's what the law of attraction is predominantly based on.

The words we use not only can hurt others as they come from within us, not only can they set someone else on a positive path or destructive path, but they can do the same to us. What we focus on our mind seeks out evidence of, even in the face of contradictory evidence.

Examples of how we use poor wording for ourselves are:

"I am hopeless at……"
"I am no good……"
"I am an idiot……"

Say this enough and you will believe it, you will upgrade to comments like:

"Well, that's just how I am……"
"It's in my blood……."
"I can't help it……."

These are the ultimate in bad words, not those other 4-letter ones you might think of.

This kind of word can hold someone back when they can develop every capability to succeed, they also give a person an excuse not to achieve or do something about whatever it is they need to face and or do.

It may leave someone falsely imprisoned in a crisis or falling short at their attempt to achieve some success.

The mind doesn't know the difference between real or fake, which is how false memories can be created, another way false memories and false neurological connections are made are through the words we consistently use.

So, in future think about what you say and the words you choose, for example:

'You are not hopeless- instead you are without useable know how at this moment',

'You are not an idiot- Instead in need of more information to complete 'x'.

There is a major difference that you can see, each word pattern yields a different feeling and attitude and therefore a different set of decisions and actions.
Which would you rather be, *Dumb* or *short on useable knowledge which you are perfectly capable of getting?*

We pick these habits up from mimicking our parents and others of influence, this illusion of perfection and needing to be perfect.

It is this mentality that starts us on the path of negative talk, yet this illusion of perfection is a result of people's insecurities and fear of making a mistake or upsetting the herd.

This is past down from generation to generation in ignorance and with great danger.

Perfection is not the goal in fact it's an illusion, evolvement is and that requires us to make mistakes for there lies the most golden of wisdom.

So be aware of the words you use daily and the meanings you give to things for they may be your vehicle for success, progress and happiness or your tool of destruction and eternal sadness.

Things To Do When Your Thoughts Take Over:

- **Ideal outcome visualisation.** Whilst performing slow breathing exercises/meditating, focus your mind on how you want things to be or focus on an image that represents what you want and hold it there. This helps move from the amygdala of our brain (Fight/

Flight etc) to the prefrontal cortex (executive functions/ problem solving) part.

- **Rehearsing how you want things to be.** Visualise and do it to movement (dance or exercise) or meditation as this embeds the new behavioural and feeling patterns into your nervous system, improving your chances of success by as much as 80%. I do exactly this to anchor new behavioural patterns and thoughts for my clients. This works because our brain doesn't know the difference between real and imagined.

- **Be objective.** Become the observer of your thoughts as if observing someone else living out your thoughts and positively advise and guide them. Take note of the insight you come up with and apply it to yourself.

As you will see later in the book, your thoughts can affect more than your decisions and actions; they can affect your health as well. So, you must make sure you are the master of your thoughts and not the other way around.

At some point you must relinquish your need for control, which often is an issue of confidence. You must let your actions resonate and yield some feedback, feedback that you require to know what you need to learn or do next, so that you can finally arrive at your desired destination.

You must realise that there is always more than one possibility, and you are never damned or stuck with one result or outcome.

You must endure many different results in order to rise to the ultimate result and this can't happen if you do not trust and let the universe do its job. When you don't let go or be open, it's as good as saying, "I don't want this, I don't deserve it." Openness in this case means detaching from doing the same thing over and over. Letting go, trusting, having faith and cultivating a sense of nothing to lose is how fears and limitations are dissolved.

Ultimately you come to realise that what you are letting go of is your ego and all its falsehood that you waste so much time trying to defend and hide, etc.

At that point you let your authenticity come through and it doesn't need defending or controlling. This attracts more good energy, which pushes you forward to success.

Basically, in letting go you open yourself to more possibility and opportunity increasing your chances of achieving the outcome you most desire.

You need to get real. It serves no purpose to deny you are afraid; it only feeds the fear. Fear loves denial and cowardice. When you run or deny, you are simply cementing the truth of your fear.

To get through, you have to go through, even if it's gradually or after many attempts. Always step up and eventually you will get through it. It's creating familiarity and the more familiar you get, the easier it becomes.

Take positive and affirmative action to learn from the fear. Seek the underlying truth/message, for there lies the solution. The fear itself is never the truth, instead it's the message bearer. Go beyond and understand the fear's origin, the real message and feedback.

Strategy Plan For Overcoming Fear:

- Reframe: what else can this situation mean, understand it better and deeper.

- Re-visualise: practice, rehearse, visualise.

- Plan: small steps to build you up.

- Keep learning: from others and other sources.

- Have a safety plan: know your limits, learn from each effort and expand on the next.

- Screw the safety plan: "I have beaten my fear." When you are confident, go ahead and be triumphant with no holds barred.

One last thing, fear and complacency can also create a bi-product, they can cause us to develop bad habits. These habits serve to calm us make us feel secure and in control, to give us something which may present as a blocker when you are looking to overcome a challenge or personal crisis or to achieve some sort of success.

Breaking Bad habits; removing old conditioned behaviours that hold us back.

It's plausible that as we initially begin a journey that is full of uncertainty and mystery and requires us to have essentially blind faith, that we develop some habits or these habits may be pre-existing, these are messages that can help you if you face them and be aware of them.

Due to the comforting nature of these habits they can often be in control of us as opposed to us in control of them. This is where a habit becomes something more, an addiction and addictions can prevent us from reaching our goals and indeed can destroy our lives.

(For the purposes of this material, I will keep this topic general, however addictions can be deep-rooted issues that may require professional attention and have varying effects on a person's life and those around them.)

Here are some basic guidelines to deal with bad habits…

Basic guidelines to deal with addictions/ bad habits:

Use this as your checklist if you know you may have a habit that's not empowering you:

- Acknowledge and embrace the habit- Denying it does not make it go away.

- Observe the behaviour, become a third party to it and observe it, as a mother observes her child.

- Go beyond the initial reactions and the visually obvious and ask, what am I getting from this behaviour, what do I perceive as lacking that I am getting from this habit, what's the payoff.

- Explore better alternatives, when you have established the payoff and or underlying reason for this habit, look for better more empowering alternatives in which you can get the same payoff or a more appropriate payoff from. Also attend to the issue that's causing the need for the habit.

- It is critical that the new more empowering action/habit be implemented and practiced immediately and constantly. Even enlist the back up of a good friend till you can do it on your own, practicing means being prepared to succeed, it means it becomes the new and empowering habit, done over and over again.

Practice (positive) Selfishness, this does not mean being obnoxious, self-centred etc.

What it means is, the minute you start tending and pleasing yourself and giving to yourself and not neglecting yourself you then start to truly become a valuable person to those you care about.

To positively give to yourself is to maintain yourself, to proclaim you deserve it and are worth it, and when you believe it, so will others. The scales are only level when both sides are balanced, once one side gets overburdened the scales tip, so will you if you deny yourself *for whatever reason(s)*......No, No, No.

Enough talk, time for action

Action Item 1:

Learning to break things down into workable parts and heading down the right path.

Take a situation you are currently dealing with and follow these simple steps.

1. Break your situation down into its elements.

2. How many elements are there?

3. Do the same with your emotions: break them down and list what you are feeling towards this situation.

4. Reframe the elements of your situation into more workable parts.

5. List each emotion you're feeling and why.

6. Consider <u>HOW</u> this situation is not right yet.

Action Item 2:

SAY NO TO FEAR

Dealing with the fear and procrastination that we may have.

1. Consider any fear you are feeling that may also be causing you to procrastinate about this or any situation. Describe what your fear is and why it is.

2. Proximity of feeling: close your eyes and try to feel where your fear is – is it behind you i.e. do you look over your mind's shoulder when you experience the fear or is it close in front of you/beside you or is it ahead in front of you i.e. in your mind's eye are you looking ahead when you feel the fear?

3. Wherever you find the location of your fear to be, that is where you need to focus. So let's see where you need to focus. Pick one:

   Behind you = unsure about your initial decision and need to review or reconsider all or aspects.

   In front/beside you = okay with initial decision, not worried about end result but stuck and uncertain about your next move.

   Ahead/in front of you = initial decision is fine, you know your next step but feeling a little unsure and unconfident about getting to the end desired outcome.

4. Proactively speaking, what would make this situation less frightful, what would you need to see or hear or have, etc.?

5. What or who would you need to make the above happen? E.g. education, training, consulting a professional, etc.

6. Build your action plan and start now.

Action Item 3:

Finally, what bad habits will you eliminate to achieve your goal?

Once we have broken our situation/challenge down and understood the various elements of it and familiarised ourselves with the potential emotional blockages, we can now...

4

FIND YOUR BEST PATH

Exploring the potential pathways to determine the best road to your desired destination.

When I sit with a client and work with them on their relevant situation, almost always and without fail at some point I will ask them what has become my catch question… "*What does that mean?*"

The next step to working through your challenge is to ask yourself what do each of the elements you have identified actually mean or what other explanations could there be.

This is referred to as reframing. Reframing works well as it gives you choices on how to approach your challenge and achieve your desired outcome.

The Power Of "What Does That Mean?"

So, when I ask my clients, "What does that mean?", I am asking them to step out of their own head and become the observer of the challenge and to consider other possibilities for that challenge or consider the sister question, "*What else can that mean?*"

Remember a time where a child or a friend came up to you all huffed and puffed and exploded into a story of great treachery, drama and injustice.

Now at that point you can see that, as dramatic as the situation was, there was probably more to it that meant it wasn't quite the drama it was made out to be.

Can you recall what you said to them? It may have been something along the lines of, "Do you really think 'X' had nothing better to do than to plot against you?" or "Is it really likely that stranger deliberately took the last bag of buns just to deny you your hot dogs?"

Or the all-important... *"What does that mean?"*

In fact, if you look at all the above question examples, you will see the connotation is—what does that mean or what else could be true of this situation?

Try this: Think of a recent or current challenge you have. For a moment step out of that scenario and just observe it. With what you are observing, if it was a friend or your child going through this, how would you otherwise explain the situation to them and what advice would you give them to help them through it?

Whatever appropriate advice you come up with, note it down and use it in your situation. Don't let it get too personal, rise above it and look at the greater picture.

This is the premise of my question, **what does that mean? Or what else could that mean?!!**

Once you have reframed the elements of your challenge, it's important you do the same with your feelings; you need to consider *what you are really feeling*.

Reframing feelings can also be known as *reconciliation of feelings* and it's when we go beyond the initial reaction and sensations of our feelings to understand the cause behind them.

To do this simply ask yourself this: *"What has been violated, denied or infringed upon or needs to be met and satisfied?"*

This is a great question to ask when communicating with others and when you feel yourself getting upset.

We are all responsible for how we interact with others, so if you are feeling upset, ask yourself what value or principle has been violated.

When doing this it's important you consider whether the other person knew this was important to you or whether they were even aware of your value.

It's important as part of this reframe process for you to clarify your value and find a way to help the other person understand, all whilst making sure you are also genuinely understanding them.

I will explore the fundamentals of this in more detail further in the book.

So let's use our example with John...

What does that mean?

John screwed me over—is it possible that John had no interest in screwing you over? Is it possible that John lost the paperwork accidentally and feels quite bad about it and wants to help?

What's been violated (perceived to be)?

I feel angry—my value of trust has been infringed. I feel frustrated—I need more information about the situation and solution. I feel annoyed—I have been moved into an uncomfortable position.

So once you have broken down the situation and your feelings and reframed them, you can now *reassess your course of action.*

Here is where you review and re-decide on what you will do and even the meaning you will give the whole challenge/situation.

It's important you do this with three things in mind:

1) *A solution-based focus:* This is quite straight forward—when you operate from a non-personal, non-emotional position, you seek effectiveness and therefore you look for practical solutions that move you forward.

2) *Proactively:* A big part of being solution-focused is acting proactively as opposed to reactively. Reactive behaviour is a character weakness, which says you are ruled by your external world (situation) as opposed to proactive, which is acting from a position of inner strength and acceptance that you can't often control what happens to you but you can control how you react and act.

3) *With a higher view and purpose:* This comes back to looking beyond just yourself and making it about you. Look at how you would rather the situation be and/or where you would rather be and look to making tracks (taking action) towards that.

Quite often most problems arise as a result of poor, reactive or lazy communication, which enflames a situation that could just as easily have gone a different way, also they arise in debates.

Some Tips For More Effective And Accurate Communication With Yourself And Others.

1) *Ask specifically:* describe exactly what you want to yourself and make sure you understand what you want. (We will cover this in far more detail in a later chapter.)

2) *Ask someone:* reflect off someone who can help and give you what you want and see if they can understand what you want.

3) *Create value for the person you're asking:* don't just ask for something from someone and not expect to give back. Help them to help you.

4) *Ask with focused, confident belief:* low confidence and uncertainty creates the same in the other person and that can lead to reluctance.

5) *Ask until you get what you want:* if you ask one person and it doesn't work out, ask another. Notice what feedback you're getting or not getting. Be flexible in your approach so as to open yourself up to more possibilities and opportunities.

Enough talk, time for action

Action Item 1:

Now it's time to start giving some thought to what you are really saying and where you want to end up.

The power of *"What does that mean"* is a great way to really sort through the rubble of your internal environment and reveal what you really are wanting and/or saying.

Using a current situation follow these steps:

1. Looking at your situation, after proclaiming it and breaking its elements down, ask yourself for each element: "What does that mean?" "What am I really saying here?

2. Consider other possibilities to help you reframe the elements/whole situation and ask yourself: "What else could this mean?"

3. Looking at your emotions, if this is the same situation you have worked on throughout the book, refer to your list of emotions in previous tasks and the explanation as to why. If this is a new situation, then follow previous tasks first. Ask yourself: "What does that mean?" and then: "What has been violated (perceived)?"

4. Looking at this fresh perspective, reframe your situation, your feelings, and the values you need met behind them, and construct a more positive and proactive communication approach. This is to be used moving forward as you deal with the situation and others involved in it.

*Remember when putting this stage together to: a) be solution focused, b) be proactive and c) operate with a higher purpose/view.

So now that we have found some potential paths, we can....

5

CLEAR THE WAY ON THE RIGHT PATH

Once we have established a sense of direction, we need to now start clearing a path to our desired destination or defining that which we want.

The Power of Planning and Strategy.

Before we start on this chapter here is an important consideration, something you must understand.

Procrastination is suffered by many, it's when you just can't decide, just aren't sure which way to go or option to take.

Quite often the result is whatever was wanting to be done gets put off or people settle for something less.

Procrastination occurs due to an absence of knowledge/know how which reduces confidence and creates a sense of uncomfortable uncertainty and or fear. It's how so many dreams and success die unnecessarily.

Another reason so many people don't achieve the outcomes they want or achieve as much as they could and may often feel like the universe is working against them is because they leave things to luck. A lack of purpose and direction with a lack of clear outcome and a viable way of achieving it means most people most of the time will be unlucky.

The irony of it all is that all the above can be eliminated and your outcomes be turned more to your favour through creating a plan and or strategy.

A plan is for creating an event or outcome a strategy is for how to get there, to achieve it.

A plan or strategy provides a number of critical elements to us:

1. It helps us work out what to do

2. It allows us to know where we have a lack of knowledge and need to do some research

3. It helps us define our desired outcome

4. It creates the path between where we are and where we want to end up

5. It creates clarity and therefore confidence and certainty

All plans should be disciplined but also flexible so as to allow for adjustments along the way as we learn and see more we realise more which means some changes may need to be made along the way.

Having a plan or strategy is critical as it gives us more power over our outcomes, it gives us knowledge to make the right decisions and take the right actions. Furthermore, it helps us deal with the challenges ahead smarter.

A plan builds confidence and also helps to attract the right people and circumstances for what you want to achieve as opposed to leaving things to chance or even worst just walking away leaving you wishing and then also wondering *'what if?'*

You now have a pretty good handle on your situation, your feelings, more positive meanings for what you're experiencing.

Where to from here?

Now comes the fun part of defining exactly what you want or, as I like to put it, what is your **desired destination?**

You see, simply stating what you want is similar to our example earlier of trying to eat a burger in one go. It's not easily doable, your mind can't grasp it well enough for us to take action on it.

Let's use an example to better understand. A common *goal* people have is to make more money, so a person says, "I want to make more money." That seems straightforward enough, so they get handed a dollar and they have more money, yet they are still upset and poor.

Can you see the issue with their *proclamation?* It was too broad and unstructured with no strategy or purpose. Your brain and in fact yourself cannot act on that and so you get nowhere.

There are a number of elements to discovering and understanding what you want and why you want it. It's important to know these as they will help you better connect with your purpose and motivation for wanting what you want.

Also, it will help with being able to start on your goal and build the right strategy, an intelligent strategy with intelligent targets along the way.

The First Step To Clearing A Path Is:

Simply Stating What You Want In Its Simplest Form

So, if you use the 'quitting job to start a business' example, you might say, "I want to have my business set up and have some regular weekly customers."

This means you are effectively making a basic proclamation, like earlier, except now it's about the future and which way you want to go, as opposed to something that is a wish or idea. It's a starting point.

You are giving shape to your goal(s), regardless of what type of outcome it may be. For example, a response or acknowledgment, an achievement and so forth.

Understanding What A Goal Is

Goal, it's such a frequently used word but what actually are goals?

'A goal is a target or a destination; it's our compass for growth and achievement'.

You need goals because they give you a sense of direction and purpose and act as your tool for evolving in life. If you didn't have goals, even subtle ones, you would not get out of bed, perhaps not even wake up.

So, what makes a goal worth chasing, and how can we know if a particular goal is right for us?

Not all goals are worth pursuing, you have to know when a goal is serving you and worth pursuing and when to let it go or change it.

Three Factors Of A Goal Worth Proceeding With

It needs to be:

1) *Current* – the goal as it stands should be accurate with what you want, believe and feel within yourself today.

2) *Relevant* – make sure you have not outgrown it and should be putting a better goal in its place or slightly adjusting its current form or timing.

3) *Inspiring* - the goal should fire you up, it should compel you from within to pursue it.

Once you have established your goal, it's a good idea to further bolster your chances of achieving it. There are couple of ways to do this: writing a goal down or telling someone about it will further improve your chances of achieving that goal. Announcing it is like setting it in stone, because then if you get lazy with your goal and even if you justify the laziness, it's hard to save face.

However, it is also important that you be careful who you tell.

They must be:

1) *Trustworthy:* The person you confide in needs to be more than just a friend, they should be a confidant and respect your privacy and trust in what you are sharing with them.

2) *Supportive:* In this case supportive means they are willing to take on the role you are asking of them and actually support you. This generally means trust you that you know what you are doing and have the ability to achieve this.

3) *Understanding:* I believe a prelude to compassion is understanding and in this case, it's understanding that there are deep-seated reasons for doing what you want to do, and also understanding that there will be challenges and stumbles along the way. This person is able to step into your shoes, to see things from your perspective and support you from that point of view,

4) *Willing and strong enough to hold you to it*: This is perhaps one of the most crucial attributes of a buddy, the ability to call you out on your own stuff and excuses, and hold you responsible for your results and persistence. It's no good engaging a buddy that when you have your first weak moment they let you off the hook with a pat on the back and tell you, "Never mind, at least you gave it a go." HOG WASH!

A goal needs to serve you and help you grow and move forward. If your goal(s) is not doing this consistently, then a review is necessary otherwise you will put it a side like many new year's resolutions.

Why So Many Fail To Achieve Their Goals And How To Build Your Vision For Success

Having observed myself and others, I noticed certain patterns in the non-achievement of goals.

There are five main reasons (in my opinion) why people don't achieve their goals:

1) *The goal is too big initially and so you don't know where to start, it's too overwhelming:* We have all done this at some point – you have an idea, or a vision and you get excited. You then set yourself a goal around achieving that vision. The only thing is in your excitement you set the goal so big that it isn't achievable, because it's so overwhelming you don't even know where to start. An example of this would be wanting to drop 30kgs of weight in a month without having ever exercised or dieted before. You get discouraged and retire the goal to the 'Goals Graveyard', also known as 'One day'.

2) *No action plan/strategy:* If making the goal too big initially is not enough, you don't plan or set a strategy on how you will achieve the goal. It's almost like you expect you will get there in one big move, but that does not work; all journeys have steps and stages.

3) *The goal is poorly defined, it's too broad:* If a goal is too broad, it's poorly defined and therefore not clear on what is really wanting to be achieved (as we have seen earlier in the book). A classic example of this is the person who says I want more money but is never able to attract it. The goal is too broad in that it does not clarify how much more money the person would

like, and how they would like to do it and what the targets would be along the way. You see, in its broad form of 'I want more money', a dollar handed to them would achieve that goal, but chances are they wouldn't be happy as they really had something different in mind. Being specific and detailed is critical to achieving your goals.

4) *Not a compelling enough 'Why', no real reason/purpose:* We covered this in some detail earlier, but it deserves a second mention. Many people see the glamorous side or the reward end of achieving in life but are often clueless to the difficulties and challenges that can present themselves along the way. Many of these challenges can be tough, tedious and time consuming, requiring patience, persistence and sacrifice. If you are to go through that, there'd better be a good reason for it, in fact there would have to be a '*no other option will do*' reason to go through the process and challenges. In other words, there has to be a meaningful and compelling purpose to want the final result.

5) *Emotions and/or ego get in the way of clear thinking and action:* It is very easy to fall into the trap of thinking the world revolves around you, when, in fact, it never really does. You get so set in what you want and how you want it that you forget to bend with the flow. Effectively you give the universe an ultimatum and it often backfires in your face. The path you see for achieving your goal may not be the best one, or your journey may take you down a different path to achieving your goal. Maybe the goal itself may alter. If you become too stubborn and set in your ways, you

will walk away from the goal before you ever achieve it virtually every time. Be flexible and maintain 'bigger picture' awareness about yourself.

That said, I believe out of the five reasons mentioned above one is the most important and I feel the need to highlight it. I believe the other four reasons could be overcome more easily if this reason is resolved.

The reason why many fail and don't achieve their goals or resolutions comes down to just one factor:

The 'WHY' was not compelling enough, it was weak in conviction and reason.

The 'WHY' needs to be strongly compelling and backed by a true and congruent purpose.

The definition of compelling is —it's NOW, not in a few years or even a few months, it's very close in proximity, therefore real enough.

> E.g. *If I don't lose weight immediately, I won't be able to have children now*

> vs.

> *If I don't change my lifestyle now, I may have diabetes in the future and my relationship may suffer some day.*

The compelling 'WHY' is powerful, which means it's far more uncomfortable not to act than it is to act. It also means there is no other choice for moving forward on whatever it is you are wanting to achieve, etc.

Most people fail because their conviction is weak; they have not found a compelling enough reason to do what they said they would do. There was no push as to why they should act and go through the change. *The way things are, regardless of consequence, is still too comfortable and familiar to get rid of and change.*

The 'WHY' is not real enough, it's not in close enough proximity, so the compulsion to act is weak or non-existent.

So, discovering your compelling 'WHY' is critical to your success, to achieving your desired results. Think of it as this: Your compelling 'WHY' is you giving yourself a powerful and positive alternative to move towards a preferred outcome and therefore having to move from where you are. Giving yourself that alternative, that 'why', is paramount.

So how do we do that?

Six Quick Steps To Changing NOW And Finding Your Compelling Why:

1) *Get real:* Many think it's a sign of weakness to admit things aren't right, but that's because they don't have the courage to step up to the truth. See things as they are, but don't make them worse than they are; catastrophising and aggrandising achieves nothing.

2) *Identify the problem areas:* Break the issues down to manageable pieces, be specific. Bombarding yourself with a giant problem is like trying to eat a whole burger in one go. As you now know, that doesn't work. Instead,

you break problems/challenges down into chewable pieces to enable you to not only understand the challenges better, but also why they occurred. This can help you find the right actions/solutions with more clarity and a greater chance of success.

3) *Be clear about why your current situation needs to change:* What are the costs or potential costs of continuing with this current situation?

4) *Create your alternative:* How would you rather or prefer things to be? What would you prefer to wake up to and how will you know you have achieved this? We will explore this element in more details further in the book.

5) *What is the payoff from taking action towards achieving this?* Come up with a minimum of 20 reasons why you <u>must</u> commit to this. The more reasons you find, the stronger your conviction. To have strength, they must be your reasons and they have to be real.

6) *Plan to win and start now:* Start planning your journey and don't wait. Make time, research, vow to every day dedicate some time to achieving your goal/change.

As you progress on your journey and more clues and pieces of the puzzle are revealed, you evolve and so does your goal(s).

You must regularly check in with yourself and confirm the <u>accuracy</u>, <u>relevance</u> and <u>currency</u> of your goal. You must be flexible with the result because what was true yesterday, may not be applicable today or it may have evolved.

You must be ready to make some adjustments and upgrades on your goal(s) or you may be chasing something that you don't want or is not the right outcome for you and you will lose interest or underperform.

Now you have a general idea of what you want, you need to break it down into its elements, but unlike before where you looked for elements that were part of an event that had happened, here you need to do some psychic work.

The Second Step To Clearing A Path Is:

To Know Exactly What You Mean About What You Want, Uncovering And Defining Specifically and Understanding Why:

Ever heard someone say they want something and in their eyes, you could see there was some confusion or a sense of uncertainty?

This is because, although they state something they want, they aren't really sure what they are asking for or they're not being specific enough in their request in order to be able to act on it or to know when they have achieved it.

Let's take a common example of someone who states they want to have more money—would they be satisfied if someone handed them a dollar? Technically that is more money but we both know they would not be happy.

So, understanding the elements of what you want is critical for creating it and attracting it into our lives— you must get clear, detailed and certain.

This can be a bit hard to do from your present position so to help you, consider this: *if you went to bed tonight and suddenly your bed was a time machine and when you woke up in the morning you were at some point in the future where you had truly arrived at your desired destination, what would you have to see, feel, have, to know you had succeeded? How far into the future would that be?*

Once you have put together as many specifics as possible, place them into a cohesive vision and then proclaim that vision; own it with a two-paragraph mission statement.

What Is A Mission Statement?

A mission statement is a half-page statement of purpose and direction. It's a claim to a specific goal/outcome.

A mission statement lets those who read it, including the author, know what the purpose and reason behind it is for those abiding by it. It gives a full description of the promise and goal, known as the mission.

It is the common denominator for all actions and decisions made by the person (or persons) to whom the mission statement belongs.

Place your mission statement on your wall, on a vision board, somewhere you can refer to it daily and do not let one day pass without having done something towards the achievement of that vision.

The Power Of Vision Boards

As we talked about earlier, the R.A.S is the part of the brain that stores a lot of our subconscious thoughts and also the part of the brain that seeks out that which we are thinking or focusing on the most.

Consider a vision board to be your external R.A.S. It's either some butcher's paper or a cork board or something similar where you put images and words representing what you truly want in your life.

You can put up any images and words that you want and build a picture that most resonates with where you want to get to in your life, with a particular goal. This creates a powerful focal point and a powerful line of thinking.

Your vision board must be consulted daily to keep your thoughts detoxed and on the greater picture.

Characteristics of an effective vision board:

1) You are able to keep it on your wall or somewhere in clear sight.

2) You can stick or pin onto it as many images and pictures of things you want to attract into your life.

3) You review it daily.

4) It's updateable – if something is achieved or no longer resonates with you, you can remove that image and replace it with something that does.

5) It sparks a flame of inspiration in you to keep going. When you are putting your vision board together, it will also help you get specific with what you want. You can only gravitate and proceed towards that which is clear to you.

But what if you don't know what you want?

In any situation, and certainly if it is *Personal Internal,* you may realise that you just don't know what you want. This can be due to a number of factors.

The two main blockages that can affect your ability to determine what you want that I will highlight in this book are *disconnection from your authentic self* and *not knowing what your values and principles are.*

Connecting To Your Authentic Self

In almost all seminars I have attended, they have said what you must do first is find your passion (more or less).

So, I asked myself, "Petros, what are you passionate about?" and a few things came to mind but none were all that compelling. I realised I didn't really know, but more profound was the realisation that I didn't know my passions because I didn't know who I was.

More messages are delivered to us today than any other time in history.

'The average eight-year-old today will have received more messages in their eight years of life than their grandparents would have received throughout their whole lives'.

How many people are you? With so much information and social and familial expectation, is it any wonder we lose ourselves. How many masks do you wear day to day?

> A mum (in herself she has many masks), a manager, a son, a father, a customer, a negotiator, a petrol station attendant, a hipster, a sporty person, a taxpayer, a cook, a caretaker, the list goes on...

With so many masks we are required to wear, what does the face under them, the authentic face, actually look like?

Your authentic face is who you really are *when no one is looking, and you don't have to play a particular role and you are completely relaxed and in your own element* – this is your authentic self.

How do I find my authentic self?

I believe the answer to this question comes down to asking yourself six simple questions that will help you sort through the masks and the dirt.

1) *Do you know how many masks you wear from day to day, how many people you are to the world?*

The purpose of this question is two-fold: firstly, to bring you awareness that in most cases you are being a persona, a character in your day-to-day interactions and dealings. And secondly, it's to get you to think about how many personas you play or masks you wear.

2) How often do you take them off (if ever)?

For some of us, we never stop being something to someone and often that is at the expense of being ourselves for ourselves and the people around us. Do you ever stop and just 'not be' a persona? Do you ever connect with that true sense of 'You'?

*3) What does the face under them look like?
   Have you seen it lately?*

This is really about asking the question "If you aren't checking in with the real 'you', when will you?" Can you describe who you are, what you are truly passionate about, <u>that</u> particular something that is for you and no one else?

*4) When do you mostly cover that face up?
   Under what circumstances?*

There are many reasons we mask our true self (that in itself is a book on its own), but if you were to stop and think about it, when do you most hide your true self? Is there ever a time when you don't? This is a good way to truly learn about yourself and where you feel most weak or vulnerable or afraid or ashamed and so on.

*5) If you were to take an educated guess, why would you
   say you cover your authentic face?*

It can be quite profound and even overwhelming working through the above four questions, especially if you had not realised you had lost yourself? But this is a critical part of the exploration process. Understanding why you hide your true self can let you discover areas you need to work on in yourself, your self-esteem and your confidence and it can also help you to rejuvenate yourself.

6) **When all masks are off and you are free, what do you do and/or yearn for the most?**

You may at times take the masks off or, after asking the first five questions, you may find you are making some changes and are able to at times take off the masks, or at least it may start to feel like that.

Observe yourself and what you do in those moments, what you enjoy doing or reading that relaxes you, that gives you a deep sense of pleasure and satisfaction. It's important that you look at activities and things that are all about you and your satisfaction and pleasure and fulfilment, not anyone else's.

Building Power and Momentum In Your Authentic Self

When you finally uncover your authentic self, you will experience significant and empowering changes within yourself; it will be like a weight has been lifted off you.

You will find that you will feel the need to defend yourself less, be more comfortable in yourself and what you do, and be able to connect more with what you want in your life and feel great about it.

Your relationships will also improve, people will react differently to you. You will attract better relationships and a better calibre of people and cleanse away the ones that no longer serve or empower you.

This, however, takes some practice, so we need to build and keep the momentum and in return, give strength and power to our authentic self so as not to lose it again.

There are six things we can do towards this.

1) *Think of between one and three ways you could incorporate these yearnings and activities more in your life?*

    As with most things that have some worth, you need a plan and in this case you need to make a plan of inclusion to condition yourself. This is a question designed to make you think about a few ways you can incorporate the new you and the things that give life to the real you into your everyday life.

2) *Can you think of five good things that can come about by taking off the masks or bringing more of your authentic self to the surface?*

    Here is where you really start to understand why being your authentic self is far better than being lost in the many personas you can become. What are the benefits for you and for those around you.

3) *How would that change your everyday life for you?*

    It's important you visualise the positive change possibilities and the freedom that comes with being true to yourself. You want to see in your mind's eye all the great changes and the good they bring, and there will be many.

4) *How would that change things with your relationships, work, home? How could you help those in these areas grow with you in understanding and acceptance, even when resistance may initially come through?*

Always remember that your visions are your visions and in making that transition to living more authentically, it is possible that those around you, the people you care about may not be sure of what's going on.

They may feel concerned, although in most cases they feed off your positive energy as you become happier. In any case, it pays to talk with the people in your life that matter and explain to them, help them to understand and feel assured that you are fine, in fact better than ever.

This may actually inspire them to do the same and rise up with you in living a better and more authentic life.

5) *What do you need to let go of/change to facilitate this positive transformation?*

The journey to your authentic self may bring up some internal struggles or matters that will need attending to. Sometimes the masks you wear are as a defence against something that's making you uncomfortable.

The mask may act as a wall between you and that issue, often giving you an excuse to keep putting off dealing with it.

It is important you stop running from these issues and address them; there is a relief and a freedom in doing so. The sooner you deal with whatever it is, the sooner it will be behind you.

6) *What are the positive alternatives you would then have to add and incorporate into your life to facilitate this positive transformation?*

   Finding your authentic self also means at some point you will need to do some spring cleaning in your life, get rid of things—activities and habits and even people—that no longer serve you and replace them with more empowering alternatives. It would be beneficial to sit and design how you want your life or aspects of it to run and execute the new design consistently. Change anything that's not working but be consistent and persistent.

Connecting to your authentic self can be described as being reborn but I prefer to look at it as coming out of a deep sleep and truly living; living congruently, meaningfully and with purpose, and being truly happy.

Discovering your authentic self is the first aspect to being able to truly discover and define what you want and why.

Let's now look at the second aspect:

Knowing Who You Are Is Also Knowing Your Values and Principles

Two other very important keys to finding yourself, uncovering the blueprint to your success in life and helping you to know what you want and define it are your values and principles. *What is a Value?* It is a standard or a code you deem to be most important for living a good, purposeful and true life.

What is a Principle? It is the actions or act you perform and/or decisions you make and keep for the purpose of living up to your values.

Values and principles are the very materials of how you choose to live and the major influences of your decisions and actions; they are your moral compass.

Your values are initially developed when you are growing up, and similar to your beliefs, you learn a lot of your values through your family circle.

Like your beliefs, however, your values need to be checked and reviewed to ensure they are definitely yours and represent and are current with who you are.

What happens when your values and principles no longer feel right or empower you?

- You change them—as you evolve so too may your values and principles.

- Holding on to old values simply prevents you from moving forward and creates conflict and resistance within your daily internal and external life.

Our purpose or mission statement is dictated by *your values,* which determine what is important to you.

So how do you develop and review your values and make sure you are living congruently with what *you* truly believe and feel?

How To Find, Define And Review Your Values

Finding your values is all about searching for certain patterns in four critical areas of your life by asking certain specific questions.

The four areas of your life that I feel help you define and find what your values are:

- *the inner sanctum,*
- *the financial realm,*
- *the global environment and*
- *the social circle.*

I split these into what I call 'The Values Quadrant', designed to help you find, define and review your values.

The quadrants are as follows:

The Inner Sanctum: This is yourself, your inner environment and effectively the foundation for the other three critical areas of your life. It's where you form your deepest values and views towards yourself and life, and what you base most of your actions and decisions on.

The Inner Sanctum questions:

- What do you mostly fill your home space with?

- Where are you most disciplined and organised?

- What activities do you spend most of your energy on?

- What internal conversations do you mostly have with yourself?

- What future do you see for yourself?

- What conversations do you have at home with others?

The Financial Realm: This is where you develop your views and relationship with and through money. It's here that you also form your wealth or lack of it. How you spend and save determines your values towards all things money, both on a personal and global level.

The Financial Realm questions:

- What's your biggest current belief about money?

- What do you mostly spend your money on?

- Do you have a financial strategy in place?
- Do you invest any money and, if so, why?
- Do you treat yourself and, if yes, how often?

The Global Environment: Here is where you find your views and values in and through events of all types from around the world. Here you start to form a wider view of the world and your relationship to it.

The Global Environment questions:

- What two events happening in the world at the moment are you interested in and do you feel somewhat passionate about?
- Why do those events move you and interest you?

The Social Circle: The people you hang out with predominantly and your relationship and commitment to them help you further understand what you value and where you place value.

The Social Circle questions:

- How often do you catch up with friends?
- What do you talk to them about mostly?
- What do they talk to you about (where you are interested) most consistently?
- Who do you hang out with the most and why them?

All these show you what you find most important in your life and are willing to commit the most to at any stage in your life. It helps you understand who you are and why you do what you do. It also allows you to review and change anything that's not working for you.

Knowing the four quadrants is not enough; you need to know the right questions to work through to get to your values and/or to make the improvements you need.
The questions in each quadrant are designed specifically to help you arrive at what is truly most important to you.

An easy reference guide: **The Values Quadrant**

The Inner Sanctum questions	**The Financial Realm questions**
What do you mostly fill your home space with?	What's your biggest current belief about money?
Where are you most disciplined and organised?	What do you mostly spend your money on?
What activities do you spend most of your energy on?	Do you have a financial strategy in place?
What internal conversations do you mostly have with yourself?	Do you invest any money and, if so, why?
What future do you see for yourself?	Do you treat yourself and, if yes, how often?
What conversations do you have at home with others?	
What two events happening in the world at the moment are you interested in and do you feel somewhat passionate about?	How often do you catch up with friends?
	What do you talk to them about mostly?
Why do those events move you and interest you?	What do they talk to you about (where you are interested) most consistently?
	Who do you hang out with the most and why them?
The Global Environment questions	**The Social Circle questions**

A simple reference to help you develop your values

Once you have answered these questions, it's important to then look through your answers and start recognising your values as at this moment.

This does not necessarily mean that they will be your actual values moving forward, they are just your values right now. Truth is you may find some of them are outdated or just not working for you anymore and they may be the cause of your stagnancy and poor outcomes in your life.

So how do you build your values for success in your life?

Looking over your answers, what values or views do you notice? List these even if they repeat throughout the four quadrants.

This list represents your overall values; however you may find there are some values that show up a few times in more than one area. Take these dominant values and list them separately.

These represent your most dominant values, your top three to five values that are currently driving you in your life.

It's time to assess them and ask the big question, "*Am I being served by these values anymore or are they contra to my current wants, dreams and success?*"

If your answer is no, then you can keep them and refer to them when faced with difficult decisions or situations where you may feel unsure as to what you should do.

If your answer is yes, they are disempowering you and you simply need to consider how they are holding you back and what would be a better value you could put in their place.

Whatever you replace becomes your new value, congruent with who you are and what you want today.

Keep your values handy and refer to them often; it's these values that will help you out of a moment of moral and conscious crisis and make you more effective and stronger, both internally and in life.

Finding The Gaps

I have found with both myself and my clients that doing a **Gap Analysis** can be a powerful tool. Quite often you end up finding that either you are not as far off as you thought or that you have more options than you initially thought.

A gap analysis is simply looking at the reality of where you are and where you want to be, and establishing your proximity by way of estimating the gap between the two places. However, it's also about finding where your strengths and weaknesses are, thus giving you a clearer view of what you might need help with or what you might need to outsource and/or research.

Seek the knowledge and guidance you need—you know what to do even when you don't know what to do.

You always know something you can do even when you know nothing.

In the past when you needed to find out some information, what did you do? You went out in search of it, whether it was finding someone who knew what to do or somewhere that had the information. In this day and age with the availability of the Internet, the world is available to all of us.

> *All you need is the will to take action and go out and look for the information you need, to learn something new that will help you achieve your goals.*

All journeys have a first step, but no journey is ever started until the first step is physically taken.

Where And How You Can Go And Get *Knowhow*

Here is a small list of where and how you can get answers to what you don't know but need to learn.

- Ask your inner circle – you may just be surprised at what your friends know, or who they know.

- Take stock of yourself, cut yourself some slack – what and or who do you know that could help you get a start? Who/What are your assets?

- Seek professional services – fee based or volunteered, etc., there are many out there with the knowhow that are willing and able to help you and at varied rates, sometimes even free.

- The Internet is quite possibly one of the greatest creations of all times. It means you can do just about anything from your home in your pyjamas. It is an infinite source of information and ideas.

- Courses – check institutions that offer short courses or off-campus studies; engage your local community centre, they often have great courses you can do to learn and grow your knowledge, and for low fees as well. Often for those on welfare your welfare agency may subsidise you to learn, as it means you may get off welfare sooner – take advantage of this.

- Seek and/or ask someone who is already where you want to be and mimic them. The best way to learn how to do or be that which you want, is to ask someone doing it well already and mirror them.

Only compare yourself to your former self and no one else. Too many people compare themselves to others and create a sense of inadequacy, not really knowing if what that person is showing is real or not knowing that

They too were once where you are now. What you see is never a guarantee of truth and never a confirmation of what those you compare yourself to have been through to get there; learn from, don't judge.

Not knowing is not an excuse, at least not anymore. If you truly want or need to know and you are serious about achieving your goals, you have plenty of avenues for getting your information.

Building knowledge and knowhow is also a critical part in creating and fulfilling goals, like the information you seek, your goals must be effective.

Your goals are your desired destination, they are purpose and direction and should therefore not be taken or made too lightly.

So how then do you create effective goals, goals you stick to and that serve you?

We now take a look at this in a little more detail and break down all the elements of goals, how to create them and achieve them.

How To Develop The Right Goals And A Strategy For Achieving Them

Make sure you are setting achievable goals and micro goals (also known as targets) for the journey, so that progress is made. Developing focus with progress is about setting achievable goals and targets for yourself to achieve, with each one moving you closer to your desired result.

You may say it's about setting little goals along the way for each element of your preparation so as to achieve your greater goal.

But to do this there are a few things you need to take into consideration, in order for you to be successful.

Next is a simple and short system I have created, called M.A.P.S.S., (the name reflects the purpose of this goal building system), to navigate towards developing effective, achievable and appropriate goals.

The M.A.P.S.S. Process For Creating Achievable Targets/Goals

*M*otivational – Is the target or goal applicable, current and relevant to the greater result and the intention? Is there a compelling enough reason to take the actions required? Is the goal congruent with and representative of your higher self and does it motivate you highly?

*A*chievable – Is the goal reasonably achievable or is it too big and overwhelming in its current form, therefore needing to be broken down further?

*P*lanned – The goal needs to be measurable and with timeframes placed on each target's achievement, needs a plan.

*S*pecific – Is the goal specifically defined or is it too broad and requiring further defining.

*S*imple – Don't overcomplicate things. The more complex your goal, the less likely you will be to start.

You don't have to have all the answers, etc., just start and the rest will come.

Once you have created your targets, make sure you are crossing them off your list as you achieve them.

It's important you acknowledge yourself for achieving each target along the way, for you are doing better than most.

Enough talk, time for action

Action Item 1:

Connect with your authentic self

To be sure you are creating goals that are truly resonating with you deeply, you must first connect with your authentic self.

1. Do you know how many masks you wear from day to day? How many people are you?

2. How often do you take them off, if ever?

3. What does the face under them look like? Have you seen it lately?

4. When do you mostly cover that face up, and under what circumstances?

5. If you were to take an educated guess why would you say you cover your authentic face?

6. When all masks are off and you are free, what do you do and/or yearn for the most?

7. Can you think of between one and three ways you could incorporate these yearnings/activities more in your life?

8. Can you think of five good things that can come about by taking off the masks or bringing more of your authentic self to the surface?

9. How would that change your everyday life for you?

10. How would that change things with your relationships, work, home? How could you help those in these areas grow with you in understanding and acceptance, even where resistance may initially come through?

11. What do you need to let go/change to facilitate this positive transformation?

12. What are the positive alternatives you would then have to add and incorporate in your life to facilitate this positive transformation?

13. Create your image of your authentic self, based on your answers from questions 6-12 and see who you really are.

Action Item 2:

Work out your values and be guided right.

Now you have an idea of who you are, you must work out what you will stand for and what foundation you will operate from.

The questions in each quadrant are designed specifically to help you arrive at what is truly most important to you.

The Inner Sanctum questions:

- What do you mostly fill your home space with?

- Where are you most disciplined and organised?

- What activities do you spend most of your energy on?

- What internal conversations do you mostly have with yourself?

- What future do you see for yourself?

- What conversations do you have at home with others?

The Financial Realm questions:

- What do you mostly spend your money on?

- Do you have a financial strategy in place?

- Do you invest any money and if so, why?

- Do you treat yourself and if yes how often?

The Global Environment questions:
- What two events happening in the world at the moment are you interested in and do you feel somewhat passionate about?

- Why do those events move you and interest you?

The Social Circle questions:

- How often do you catch up with friends?

- What do you talk to them about mostly?

- What do they talk to you about (where you are interested) most consistently?

- Who do you hang with the most and why them?

So, what are your values that will project you forward?

- Looking over your answers, what values or views do you notice? List these even if they repeat throughout the four quadrants.

- This list represents your overall values; however, you may find there are some that show up a few times in more than one area. Take these dominant values and list them separately.

- These represent your most dominant values, your top three to five values that are driving you currently in your life.

- It's time to assess them and ask the big question, "*Am I being served by these values anymore or are they contra to my current wants, dreams and success?*"

- If your answer is no, then you can keep them and refer to them when faced with difficult decisions or situations where you may feel unsure as to what you should do.

- If your answer is yes, they are disempowering you and you simply need to consider how they are holding you back and what would be a better value you could put in its place.

Action Item 3:

Review or build the skeleton of a goal.

You may have a goal you have been working on for a while or be in the early stages of setting a goal, let's make sure it's the right goal.

Is your goal:

Current: Current with how you are today?   Y / N

Relevant: Have you outgrown the goal as it is? Y / N

Inspiring: Does the goal truly excite you and move you to consistent action? Y / N

If you answered "No" to any of these three points, review and or redesign your goal until you can honestly answer "Yes".

Action Item 4:

Build your goals and targets.

Using my M.A.P.S.S. System, refine, fine tune or create your goal and then create achievable targets for your journey.

Motivation – What is the compelling reason(s) to achieve this?

Achievability – Break the goal down into achievable parts.

Planning – Build measures and timeframes for each target, as well as your overall goal.

Specificity – Make the goal specific, defined and not too broad.

Simple – Is your first move one you understand and can begin with relative ease? If not, rework it.

Once you have created your targets, make sure you are crossing them off your list as you achieve them. It's important you acknowledge yourself for achieving each target.

Action Item 5:

Write your mission statement and begin building your vision board.

Once you have cleared a path and destination, you can now...

6

FORGE YOUR WAY FORWARD

Working out your arrival (or the 'what's and how's') and breaking down the different stages on your path.

One of the biggest hurdles to starting on the journey to a goal and achieving it is procrastination. Procrastination can be a sign of low self-confidence, which often comes when you're not sure of what to do.

Depending on the endeavour, it can be quite overwhelming and confusing when you consider what to do or even how to get started, and in most cases people would rather walk away from the goal.

This can cause stress and internal conflict, especially when the goal is one you really wish to achieve but feel helpless towards doing so.

When you think of what you want, you think backwards, meaning you go straight to the end result. You don't start from the creation of the outcome. Therefore, beginning at the start so as to end up at the desired outcome is not as easy as it looks, as it's unknown and un-manifested at this stage.

That's why I recommend starting at the end and heading to the beginning; think of it as reverse engineering your goal to find the best way to start and achieve it.

When I am sitting down with someone to help them work out their course of action, I work backward with them using a process I call **Deconstruction.**

What on earth am I on about? When you set a goal, you base it on what you want, you see your arrival or preferred destination, your end goal first. Therefore, it makes sense that the end is the best starting point when it comes to setting out the journey and your targets.

As I see it there are five stages to navigate through and they are (and I note them backward deliberately):

- **Arrival**
- **Implementation**
- **Preparation**
- **Needs establishment**
- **Decision**

Let's look at each of these now in a little more depth.

By starting with the end as Step One and working backwards to the beginning at Step Five and by following this method, you will have your action plan mapped out.

You will know how to get started and what your first move should be, thus eliminating any procrastination.

Arrival: You have established your arrival – this refers to your end result, your destination. The more detail you come up with, the better; however, it is not critical to have all the detail. A decent picture of how and what you want will suffice.

The *arrival* stage is simply the dream, the vision of what you want to be happening and how you want yourself to be.

Here, it is critical you don't hold back, be what I call '*positively selfish*', it's your life, your vision, have fun with it!

Implementation: The name says it all, it's the step (or steps) just before having what you want; the final sequence of events that ushers you from *not quite there* to *I am there*.

Knowing your end result, what do you think you would have had to implement just before it, to arrive at your desired outcome? This is understanding, as best as possible, what you would have had to have done right before succeeding.

Look at the details of your arrival and even approximately guess what would have had to have been implemented for that to happen. The answer is in your arrival stage, which provides clarity. This whole process is about creating detailed clarity.

Preparation: Before you can start a car to drive it, a few things need to happen; you need to make sure there is petrol in it, water in the radiator, brake fluid, oil and so on. It's the same here—before you can implement something that will propel you to your desired outcomes, you need to make some preparations.

By completing the previous step, you already know approximately what you would have had to have implemented to arrive at your desired destination, so the next thing to consider is how you would have had to prepare those elements. This is to help you break down what you need to have prepared in order to have implemented the elements you listed in the implementation stage.

Needs Establishment: This part is truly amazing; it's here you go from no clue to a full list of actions you can start a.s.a.p. So, knowing now what you have to prepare, what then do you think your needs would be for getting started on your path to your desired destination?

At this stage you can now start thinking presently and with clarity and focus. This ultimately marks the first physical steps you have to take towards attaining your goal.

Grab a sheet of paper and a pen and start listing your action items. Once done, waste no time, get started as soon as you can and keep going until you arrive.

Finally, and most importantly...

Decision: Why do I have this step? Before anything can ever happen, you must decide to take the action, to seek the knowledge and make your desired destination a reality.

This decision can only be made when the reasons for doing it are so compelling that not doing it is unbearable torture.

In fact, success ultimately is a non-negotiable decision to commit to constant and positively effective actions, in order to achieve your ideal outcomes in life.

This simply means that you will no longer settle for what you have been getting, for the mediocre, the everyday. It means that you will allow yourself to expand to new levels and break the illusions of limitations that have controlled the lives of you and many others throughout the world, and you will take the actions that are required to succeed and never stop.

I have provided you with a simple example of this process to better clarify what I mean and how it works, and so you can also model it in real life.

A Basic Example Using The Deconstruction Method

Scenario: Losing weight as the end goal

Arrival stage: Lost 20 kilos (45 pounds) and able to wear my high school jeans and run two kilometres (1.4 miles) all in three months.

Implementation stage: Completed three months of gym and personal training and made at least one successful attempt at a two-kilometre run. Have an eating plan that is catered for days in advance with full cooking sessions twice a week and regular review and meditation making it a second-nature habit.

Preparation: Schedule gym sessions at least three times a week, book at least one personal training session a week and do research at least one to two hours a week, plan my meals intake and schedule specific foods at specific times, keep my jeans out and images of what I want to achieve in view for motivation. Tell a trusted friend of my goal and ask them to hold me to my goal.

Needs Establishment: new food list, buy foods, gym membership, paid personal training, create a training schedule, buy and read some mindset books (like this book), sneakers, training clothes, pick a trusted friend.
(THIS NOW IS YOUR PHYSICAL STARTING POINT).

Decision: My compelling reasons for this are that I don't want to keep puffing out just walking a short distance, I want to attract my dream lover, I want to be able to live healthy and free from disease, I want to feel alive and start a family. I don't want to be a prisoner in my body.

Enough talk, time for action

Action Item 1:

Building your path to success.

Starting at the end and heading to the start, map your starting point and strategy for achieving a goal:

Arrival:

Implementation:

Preparation:

Needs Establishment:

Decision:

Now that you have started to make tracks, you can...

7

ARRIVE AT YOUR DESTINATION

Achieving your desired result and knowing you have actually arrived.

Many think the journey ends once you arrive, but the arrival itself is very much part of the journey and the process and has its own two critical elements to it.

It's not unheard of for people to arrive at their desired destination and not realise it because they are too caught up in the process to look and evaluate their efforts. Now there are a number of reasons why this can happen, too many for this book, but mostly it's because they don't describe their arrival beforehand to enable them to recognise it when they get there.

The First Step To Arriving Is:

Set The Scenery, Become Familiar With Where You Want To End Up:

Remember your bed that became a time machine and took you to the future? *I know, how cool would it be if your bed was a time machine? But I digress...*

Think back to the answers you came up with in answering that question and list them.

It is important that you become familiar with your answers and even elaborate further on them. I would even suggest that you find a clever way to incorporate them into your vision board. You see, the more you detail your results, the easier it will be to identify your success.

Many get so caught up in the process, they forget to stop and look to see when or if they have arrived, and they keep going wondering if they will ever make it. Set the scene, give yourself an arrival point and get familiar with it so you know when you have made it. Remember to stop and experience the journey, smell the roses!

The Second Step To Arriving Is:

Arrive Before You Leave:

What!? I hear you say, this involves a little more travelling into the future?

This part is about seeing yourself arrive and feeling what that is like, seeing yourself at your desired destination or achieving your desired result.

Visualising the end point allows you to operate from a foundation of *'I already have that which I want, and it's not out of reach.'*

But why is it so important to see it ahead of time?

The Power Of Thoughts

When you visualise something, you are thinking about it and your thoughts have great power and will set the tone of your conviction, actions and results.

Thoughts are energy and can be measured. They burn calories—it is estimated that thinking can burn up to 120 calories… I know… here we are slugging it out at the gym when we could have just thought about it!

Well, not quite! It's intense thinking that reaches those levels of calorie expenditure and nothing can replace exercise for physical fitness.

Thoughts also precede feelings and emotions—this happens so fast we often think it's the other way around but it's not; our thoughts dictate how and what we feel.

Depending on the type of thoughts we have, our body releases different kinds of hormones. For example, with positive and happy thoughts the main hormones released are serotonin and dopamine.

Negative thoughts generally release cortisol, which has a catabolic effect on your body. It can slow energy metabolism and make your internal environment toxic, leaving you vulnerable to disease.

When you are imagining yourself at your desired destination, having achieved what you wanted, you are setting your thoughts—which determine your feelings—which determine your actions and the quality of them.

Going into the future to your success also allows you to become even clearer and more familiar with what you want. You see your mind does not know the difference between real and imaginary, which is why so often dreams can feel real.

It is through this process that you are able to put yourself in a mindset of "I already have it" and can therefore move with more confidence towards the achievement of your goals.

So, how do you practice effective visualisation and bring yourself to your success, before you have even started? Good question.

On the next couple of pages, I have added a short visualisation exercise to help you see yourself arriving at your desired destination before you have even left.

Use this as often as you need to, your brain does not know the difference between real and fake, so when you see yourself as you want to be, your brain makes you feel as if it's real.

When you tune into those feelings, the behaviours are such that complement this thinking and you therefore attract more of the same.

This is a powerful technique to help you along the way to your desired destination.

Practicing Effective Visualisation

- Looking at your list from the *'What I want'* section, find a quiet place you can occupy for a few minutes.

- Read over the list then close your eyes and take five deep breaths, slowly calming yourself down, focusing on your breathing.

- Now picture yourself in comfortable surroundings of your choice, whatever appeals to you and makes you feel relaxed and comfortable.

- Then look ahead of you and notice that there, a small distance away, is your future self, the self that is realised and arrived.

- Consider for a moment how the future you: looks, is dressed, stands, breathes, and moves.

- Approach the future you—how do you feel and smell, what colours are around you? Take a few minutes to look at the future you and really take in the energy and really see how you are.

- Then stand behind yourself. It's now time to feel for a moment what it's like to be the future you. Take five more deep calm breaths and on the fifth, step into yourself, effectively becoming one with your future self.

- Now how does it feel? Take three minutes: consider you are at a group gathering—who is there and what are they saying about you?

- How are you speaking, what are you feeling and what are you wearing?

- What is true about your arrival, what is the proof in that future moment that you have arrived, what things have you attracted/manifested, who have you attracted/manifested?

- Just bask in the energy of being realised and having arrived, breathe it in, take five big deep breaths and really absorb your arrival.

- Now as you start to relax, consider one power word that completely describes you, the moment and your arrival. When you have done that, take a picture of that moment and write that word on it.

- Take the picture, fold it up four times and place it in your pocket. Then give thanks to your future self for letting you have a glimpse of what it's like to arrive.

- Take five more deep breaths and on the fifth breath, step out and as you do, yell out your power word.

- Once again, observe your future self, absorb their reverence and magic. Do this for a minute or so.

- Then head back to the bench you started at in the surrounding of your choice.

- Sit down and reflect on your magical experience and, when you are ready, take five deep breaths and slowly come back to the present. Take it nice and slow—if you are sitting or lying, come up slowly until you are fully present again.

- How did that feel, did it sound good, look awesome? Grab a journal and write down everything about the future you and your arrival moment.

- Reflect back on it often and recall your power word as a reminder of where you are going and what is in it for you. Even visit your future you again as often as you want.

Don't worry, I have converted this to a relaxing MP3 and you can download it from:

www.yougotthiscounselling.com.au/meditation

Things To Remember To Do And To Allow To Happen Along The Way

There are certain inevitable factors on the journey to *unlocking your internal G.P.S.* Some of these may be seen as negative or unwanted, but the truth is they are critical to a successful outcome in your life.

Regardless of what area of your life you focus on in unlocking your internal G.P.S., experiencing the following factors is crucial and they require some understanding and alternative perspective.

First Factor: Know A Lot Of Failure.

No, I have not lost my marbles and before you put this book down thinking I am crazy, know this... no one ever truly succeeded without failing. To have done so is to not have understood what success is nor truly experienced it.

Failure does not mean you are hopeless or imperfect, it does not mean you are no good and laughable. People laugh at others' failure or place pressure on people for failing because it's an excuse to mask their own insecurities, misguided fears and frustrations of not being good enough and/or of the fact that they themselves are simply afraid.

It's unfortunate that we live in a society that misrepresents what being successful, beautiful and acceptable is. It seems the more falseness you create, the better you are, but this is a lie. This is a lie that has bred over time through misguided notions and commercial agenda.

Perfectionism is a by-product of insecurity and non-self-acceptance. A common thought line of a perfectionist is, "If I am not perfect or if I don't perform perfectly, then I do not deserve... or I am not worthy... or I am not good enough", etc.

This is not successful thinking, *this is EGO and you must check the EGO, as this line of thinking misguides you and chains you down rather than sets you free to live truly and honestly fulfilled.*

Seven Ways To Subdue The EGO And Let In Success and Abundance:

1) *Don't be so precious* – you don't always have to be offended, in fact you rarely have to be, it's a decision.

2) *No, it's not a race, there is no first place* – if you always focused on beating everyone, you would never actually arrive at your own self and your success. So you beat the guy next to you, what does that really mean?

3) *Practice doing the right thing over always being right* – like gum, always being right loses its flavour and makes for very lonely company, and your way isn't the only way or always right.

4) *You don't have to be superior to someone* – superiority is a sign of inferiority.

5) *Craving more is not knowing the abundance you have* – it's telling the universe you are poor and never have enough to satisfy you, this is truly hell. It also means that

even if you got what you wanted, you probably wouldn't know it and appreciate it, because you are looking ahead for more.

6) *Your identity is not what's happened or expected of you but what you decide today* – neither the past nor others' expectations are who you are. You are who you feel in your heart and gut, today. You control this, not external circumstances. Others' expectations are their own reflections of who they wish they were or even are at that moment.

7) *Let go of your reputations* – inner authenticity is what's real and makes you- **you**. Reputations are a dime a dozen and change with the weather; trying to keep up with them is futile and a waste of life.

So do not be afraid of failure for it's not your enemy, instead it's your guide to what you need to be doing.

Failure is valuable feedback that leads the astute and open person to the best way to accomplish their task.

Failure is critical to success as long as you are taking the lessons from the failure and applying them consistently in subsequent and continuous efforts at achieving your task.

Failure is trial and error, the very process of evolution and progression. Failure, therefore, is necessary to your growth, learning and development, and achievement.
The best way to use failure is in the same way a scientist performs a series of experiments and writes down their observations or *learnings*.

Once they document their learnings, they then create a fresh set of experiments using the learnings to create new and improved methods and results, until they achieve their end goal.

Failure is meant to happen as it's the greatest way we learn, it embeds information on a physical, mental and psychological level.

It is up to us how it affects us and what comes of the failure.

Eight Simple And Common-Sense Steps For How To Use Failure In Your Favour:

1) *Remove the need to judge:* Judgment is often, if not always, the result of low confidence and insecurities. This blinds you to see the bigger picture of a failure, that is to say the valuable feedback that you can gain from a failure and the clues it can give you to succeed. You must be a neutral, open-minded observer.

2) *Document and analyse/observe the whole event leading to the result*: To make proper sense of what the event, the failure and the lead up to it all mean, it is effective to write down the various elements and analyse them. This gives you a thorough and empirical rather than emotional view of the situation.

3) *Realise the result is not the be all and end all; it's about the events leading to it that matter*: Do not get too caught up in the result, instead understand what lead to it, for the answers you want that can help you move forward are there. The result is just an indicator that means nothing once you learn the lessons and start the

next effort. It is not reflective of your ability or your destiny, it's merely feedback on that specific attempt. Results are stepping-stones to the end destination.

4) *Determine what worked and understand why:* In some cases, it is possible that some things worked and some didn't. It is important to separate what worked and understand why it did.

You don't want to throw the baby out with the bath water, as the old saying goes. If something worked, it's a clue to part of the puzzle of achieving your desired outcome.

5) *Determine what didn't work and understand why:* Some of the richest wisdom comes from what doesn't work for you. Most people will react with a negative and defeatist attitude, not recognising the valuable information in the elements that didn't work.

6) *Do your research and replace what didn't work with something better:* Once you know the full anatomy of your current results, you know the areas you need to investigate further and get more information on to then make an improved attempt at your desired outcome. This boosts your likelihood of achieving what you want to achieve.

7) *Reapply your efforts and test the new strategy/ method:* As with any new attempt, you apply what you have learned and yield a new set of results, which at some point will be the result you are after.

8) *Repeat the above until you have achieved or arrived at your goal:* This point is simply highlighting yet again the importance of persisting until you achieve and to never be discouraged by undesired outcomes. The moment will come where you will achieve what you want but only if you persevere.

It is important to fail on your journey to success for two reasons:

1) It's how you learn and evolve to become who you need to be to fully realise your success

2) It's the only way to overcome your fear and discomfort towards failure: the two biggest blocks to success, however you define success.

Second Factor: Repeat, Repeat, Repeat x Infinity

This is a simple rule that simply states, whatever your goal, you will not get it the first time. In fact it may take 1000 goes or more. However, if you truly want it and its worth it, how long it takes won't matter, just getting there will.

This principle is about developing *discipline and consistency*, for it's the disciplined and consistent person that makes it over the line, by skill and not by fluke. Luck has little to do with it, although present at time, luck only really exists as an acronym:

Learning **U**nder **C**orrect **K**nowledge.

'I have failed, been set back far more than I have succeeded, but I am here because of what I did with my failures'.

80% of people quit after their first or second try, and of the 20% that go beyond, 80% of them will quit just before they actually make it, effectively quitting just before the finish line.

Success is a journey and essentially, it's not only about the end result, it is also about who you become on the way there; it's a journey to another world not around the corner to the local store, so prepare for a long journey.

This means there is a lot to take in on the way and a lot of stops to ask for directions. It means doing the same right thing over and over again: Fill the tank, start the car, release the hand break, accelerate, stop, refuel and start again until you make it to where you want to be.

How long do you give a young child to learn to walk before you scrap all efforts? You don't, you keep going until the child walks and beyond on to running, and this doesn't change just because you are an adult.

You don't go to the gym once and suddenly have big muscles; it's *committed and proper repetition* that develops your ability and skill that gets you over the finish line.

Success is rarely instant and even more rarely instant and sustainable; success takes trial and error and effort. The path is not straight and not often flat and easy. It's something you really have to want to achieve and maintain your *motivation and momentum!!*

Without a doubt there will be times when your motivation will waver because the road to success (as you now know) is filled with setbacks, knockdowns and failed attempts.

So, what do you do when you are feeling discouraged, as though the wind has been knocked out of you? Below are seven simple steps I recommend and use to keep motivation and momentum alive, even when things feel heavy and as though they are going against me.

Seven Basic Principles For Maintaining Motivation And Momentum:

1) Never quit but acknowledge the reality of how things are.

2) Make alterations in your approach and actions as needed.

3) If something is not working, don't just walk away or insist on doing the same thing over and over again expecting a different result.

4) Keep energised, rested, with a breakaway activity, sometimes you will need to step away and clear your head in order to continue and avoid burn out.

5) Maintain daily contact with the achievement of your goal.

6) Stop and ask for directions—talk to people who know and can give you some direction, apply what you learn immediately.

7) Eventually you will develop a process that works best, make it fun, track progress and what works and repeat over and over and over and over and over again until you have met and exceeded your goal.

Enough talk, time for action

Action Item 1:
Fix the problems, keep cruising.

Time to review where you aren't progressing in a current situation or task and turn it around, so you can keep succeeding at your goal.

Follow the eight simple and common-sense steps for how to use failure in your favour (for definitions refer to page 162):

- Remove the need to judge. Where are things not right?

- Document and analyse/observe the whole event leading to the result.

- Determine and list what worked and understand why.

- Determine and list what didn't work and understand why.

- Do your research and replace what didn't work with something better.

- Reapply your efforts and test the new strategy/method.

- Repeat the above until you have achieved or arrived at your goal.

Action Item 2:

Follow the visualisation exercise from chapter 7, download free audio recording of the exercise from my freebies page at:

www.yougotthiscounselling.com.au/meditation

Note the elements and features of your arrival point, be familiar and then make the adjustments as per Action Item 1 and get going.

Thoughts and emotions:

FINAL THOUGHTS

I'll never forget it, waking up on the 6th of July 2007. It was meant to be a happy day, instead I felt like I'd crashed through 50 brick walls and rolled into a pool of antiseptic.

The fear and anxiety pulsing through me like an out-of-control freight train; I felt as if every second of my life I was running from Godzilla.

I was at a point of major crisis... do you know the definition of crisis? A crisis is a turning point, and I was definitely at a turning point; however, I couldn't see any turns.

It took me some time to realise this but the reason I couldn't see any turns was because I hadn't yet created any. I had the expectation that somehow something and/or someone would show me what to do.

Nothing or no-one ever showed up. It was up to me to decide what would become of me.

It was in this thought, amongst many, I realised something profound and critical about life, and that is: *Life is something we make and develop from the resources (and this includes hard times) provided to us by the infinite creations of the divine source, whatever that may be for you.*

We may not have control over circumstances, but just like how the sculptor, who can never be sure of what his lump of rock will be like, still finds the way to create their masterpiece, such is true of you and your life.

We all make decisions in our life, yet why do so many suffer or live less than they dream of?

The truth be told, it's because most people don't know what it means to make a decision, how to make a proper, empowering and positively effective decision or the elements behind such a decision.

The majority of people dispense decisions like dice at the craps table and hope, just like in craps, that the dice rolls in their favour.

In that moment control and power over their life ceases to be their own and they are at the mercy of the dealer, otherwise known as circumstance.

This was certainly true of my life until I maxed out and was in deep debt to the cosmic house. But unlike a real casino, the cosmic house gave me some clues as to what I needed to do to pay my debt and be in good solid standing... for the first time in my life.

I often said, after hearing it from a number of my own mentors, that the quality of your life is equal to the quality of your communication. I do agree with this and I would add a little bit more.

The quality of your life is dependent on the meanings you give to things, the decisions you make from those meanings and the actions you choose to take from what you have decided something means. These in truth are the three elements that make up our self-communication, which dictates our life.

To communicate well with ourselves as described above, it is equally as important that we know our true self well; it's the only way we can know what we want, what we will stand for or not. It is then we can step out of our door every day on a solid foundation and know we can handle pretty much anything and, with a clear and authentic vision, head straight to what we truly desire in our life.

It is all this that the G.P.S. system gives to you and I truly hope that you have the life-changing results from it that I had. In fact, I know you will if you just allow the process to happen for you.

There are seven simple and practical steps that you can use at any time (or all the time) in your life to make sure that the odds are no longer in favour of circumstance but in favour of you and your desired destination for your life.

In the following pages are some extra goodies I decided to pack into this book for you to further help you along your journey.

Check them out. I hope you enjoy them and get the value out of them that I know they hold within them.

Thank you, and may you live like you mean it.

Petros Galanoulis

IT DOESN'T END WITH THIS BOOK...

Keep in touch through:

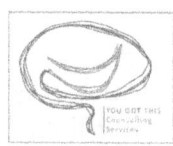 www.yougotthiscounselling.com.au

 https://www.facebook.com/YGTcounselling

Also!
Remember your MP3 of my meditation from Ch 7 😊

www.yougotthiscounselling.com.au/meditation

ABOUT THE AUTHOR

Petros Galanoulis is a trauma and life stages Counsellor & Coach, helping people solve and recover mentally and emotionally form a personal crisis, trauma or challenge.

From a young age Petros noticed that people quickly felt comfortable with him and found it easy to open up to him. He soon realised he was able to intuitively provide insights and direction beyond his years with significant results.

Based in Melbourne Australia, Petros works predominantly with individuals who are struggling through a major and difficult life transition/ trauma event such as a break-up, awakening, loss, sexual violation and so forth.

He also works with organisations and their leadership teams to help them be a positive influence and to know what to do when a staff member is experiencing a difficult life event/ transition.

With over 15-years of professional experience and over 30-years of personal experience, he developed his coaching process: The G.P.S. System.

Petros has appeared in the media in an advisory/ guiding capacity. His personal and professional mission is to be constantly looking at, and creating, different and unique ways to help those who are ready to breakthrough to a life better than they imagined and to inspire them to action and rip off the veil of illusion that is the victim mentality.

Petros holds a Master's in Counselling, his Bachelor of Psychology where he received significant credits and acknowledgement for his work and study done already in this field, Diploma of Counselling, Diploma of Life Coaching w/ NLP. Petros also studied the spiritual philosophy of Vedanta and is Reiki qualified.

Clients that have worked with Petros have been able to overcome their challenges, find their purpose or sense of direction and restructure their lives to begin living it authentically, happily and fulfilled and with new lifelong skills.

Petros is also a practical and inspirational speaker and thought provoker and can be sought and booked below.

Media enquiries to
gotasec@yougotthismentlhealth.com.au

****

OTHER BOOKS BY PETROS

REACHING FOR THE LIGHT
A Path For Deep Healing,
Forgiveness And Re-Empowerment
After Sexual Trauma

The human spirit-determined to live-can and will breakthrough even the darkest and most heinous of acts and times. A powerful journey of 6 real life former victims called 'Warriors' (male and Female) and a real-life reformed perpetrator given the ultimate ultimatum and second chance by his victim, one of the 6 warriors.

Healing, rebirth, surprise and spiritual growth.

Plus, through a 13 step, real life application process, start healing and re-build an extraordinary life after sexual trauma. This book challenges and debunks some common ideas, beliefs and brings to light some critical issues around sex and appropriate sexual conduct, such as the 3 C's of appropriate sexual conduct; for all to apply and think about and discuss around the dinner table.

Amazon bestseller

'I Did It!'
16 Mindset Secrets To Transform The Life You Have Into The Ultimate Life You Deserve

How did they do it?

Do you often wonder what is that 'One Secret' that gives certain people the extraordinary tools to transform their lives? You may think, "If I know what they are, I can create my Ultimate life too!"

In this book, you will discover 16 different secrets from successful entrepreneurs around the world, sharing their proven methods with you. It's like having 16 mentors coaching you directly.

They generously reveal the strategies, mindset, and wisdom they learned by embracing their inner strength to create their Ultimate life. You will be able to model and use the exact same tactics and create your own success in your life.

These are real people with real results. Anyone with a dream and passion can apply the secrets shared in this book and create their own success too. All you have to do is follow the step-by-step path they have laid out before you.

One year from now, you could be living your Ultimate Life, whether it is in lifestyle, career, business, love - no matter what you desire! While giving your family the best possible future!

YOUR DAILY MENTAL PIT STOP:

Some ancient wisdom to move you to take action...

"There is only ever one hurdle in life OUR SELF, so get over yourself today!"

"Our darkest hour is the bitter key that will unleash our greatness if we just let it unlock our true essence and not resist it out of fear!"

"Nothing have you; if you don't have a great relationship with yourself and your creator."

"Your death will come before the perfect moment, so stop waiting and get started NOW!"

"Success is easy: Take action, fall down, get back up, progress a little, fall down, get back up and repeat until you succeed."

"One does not truly define oneself when times are good, but only in the times where it feels impossible to get up!"